Sadlier

We·Believe ™

God Loves Us

WITH PROJECT DISCIPLE
Pray
Learn
Celebrate
Share
Choose
Live

Grade One

S® Sadlier

Nihil Obstat

Monsignor Michael F. Hull, S.T.D.
Censor Librorum

Imprimatur

✠ Most Reverend Dennis J. Sullivan, D.D.
Vicar General of the Archdiocese of New York
January 27, 2010

Acknowledgments

Excerpts from the English translation of *The Roman Missal*, © 2010, International Committee on English in the Liturgy, Inc. All rights reserved.

Excerpts from the English translation of the *Catechism of the Catholic Church* for the United States of America, copyright © 1994, United States Catholic Conference, Inc.—Libreria Editrice Vaticana. English translation of the *Catechism of the Catholic Church: Modifications from the Editio Typica* copyright © 1997, United States Catholic Conference, Inc.—Libreria Editrice Vaticana. Used with permission.

Scripture excerpts are taken from the *New American Bible* with *Revised New Testament and Psalms* Copyright © 1991, 1986, 1970, Confraternity of Christian Doctrine, Inc., Washington, D.C. Used with permission. All rights reserved. No part of the *New American Bible* may be reproduced by any means without permission in writing from the copyright owner.

Excerpts from the English translation of *Rite of Baptism for Children* © 1969, International Committee on English in the Liturgy, Inc. (ICEL); excerpts from the English translation of *Lectionary for Mass* © 1969, 1981, 1997, ICEL; excerpts from the English translation of *Rite of Penance* © 1974, ICEL; excerpts from the English translation of *A Book of Prayers* © 1982, ICEL; excerpts from the English translation of *Book of Blessings* © 1988, ICEL. All rights reserved.

English translation of the Glory to the Father, Lord's Prayer, and Apostles' Creed by the International Consultation on English Texts. (ICET)

"We Believe, We Believe in God," © 1979, North American Liturgy Resources (NALR), 5536 NE Hassalo, Portland, OR 97213. All rights reserved. Used with permission. "People Worry," © 1993, Daughters of Charity and Christopher Walker. Published by OCP Publications, 5536 NE Hassalo, Portland, OR 97213. All rights reserved. Used with permission. "Children of God," Michael B. Lynch. Copyright © 1977, Raven Music. All rights reserved. Used with permission. "Jesus Wants to Help Us," music and text © 1999, Christopher Walker and Paule Freeburg, DC. Published by OCP Publications, 5536 NE Hassalo, Portland, OR 97213. All rights reserved. Used with permission. "In the House of Our God," © 1988, 1989, 1990, Christopher Walker. Published by OCP Publications, 5536 NE Hassalo, Portland, OR 97213. All rights reserved. Used with permission. "Sing for Joy," © 1999, Bernadette Farrell. Published by OCP Publications, 5536 NE Hassalo, Portland, OR 97213. All rights reserved. Used with permission. "Share

the Light," © 1999, Bernadette Farrell. Published by OCP Publications, 5536 NE Hassalo, Portland, OR 97213. All rights reserved. Used with permission. "We Are the Church," © 1991, Christopher Walker. Published by OCP Publications, 5536 NE Hassalo, Portland, OR 97213. All rights reserved. Used with permission. "We Are the Church" was originally from "Come, Follow Me" Music Program, Benziger Publishing Company. "Advent Song," Words/Music by MaryLu Walker © 1975, 1998, 16 Brown Road, Corning, New York 14830. All rights reserved. Used with permission. "Jesus, Come to Us," © 1981, 1982, OCP Publications, 5536 NE Hassalo, Portland, OR 97213. All rights reserved. Used with permission. "Open Our Hearts," © 1989, Christopher Walker. Published by OCP Publications, 5536 NE Hassalo, Portland, OR 97213. All rights reserved. Used with permission. "We Celebrate with Joy," © 2000, Carey Landry. Published by OCP Publications, 5536 NE Hassalo, Portland, OR 97213. All rights reserved. Used with permission. "Walk in the Light," © 1996, Carey Landry. Published by OCP Publications, 5536 NE Hassalo, Portland, OR 97213. All rights reserved. Used with permission. "Children of God," © 1991, Christopher Walker. Published by OCP Publications, 5536 NE Hassalo, Portland, OR 97213. All rights reserved. Used with permission. "Awake, Arise and Rejoice!" © 1992, Marie-Jo Thum. Published by OCP Publications, 5536 NE Hassalo, Portland, OR 97213. All rights reserved. Used with permission. "Shout From the Mountains," © 1992, Marie-Jo Thum. Published by OCP Publications, 5536 NE Hassalo, Portland, OR 97213. All rights reserved. Used with permission. "We Come to Share God's Special Gift," © 1991, Christopher Walker. Published by OCP Publications, 5536 NE Hassalo, Portland, OR 97213. All rights reserved. Used with permission. "Walk in Love," © 1990, North American Liturgy Resources (NALR), 5536 NE Hassalo, Portland, OR 97213. All rights reserved. Used with permission. "Joseph Was a Good Man," music and text © 1999, Christopher Walker and Paule Freeburg, DC. Published by OCP Publications, 5536 NE Hassalo, Portland, OR 97213. All rights reserved. Used with permission. "Malo, Malo, Thanks Be to God," © 1993, Jesse Manibusan. Administered by OCP Publications, 5536 NE Hassalo, Portland, OR 97213. All rights reserved. Used with permission. "Alleluia No. 1," Donald Fishel. © 1973, WORD OF GOD MUSIC (Administered by THE COPYRIGHT COMPANY, Nashville, TN). All rights reserved. International copyright secured. Used with permission.

William H. Sadlier, Inc.
9 Pine Street
New York, NY 10005-1002

ISBN: 978-0-8215-6401-1
3456789 WEBC 15 14 13 12 11

The Subcommittee on the Catechism, United States Conference of Catholic Bishops, has found this catechetical series, copyright 2011, to be in conformity with the *Catechism of the Catholic Church*.

The Sadlier *We Believe* Program was drawn from the wisdom of the community. It was developed by nationally recognized experts in catechesis, curriculum, and child development. These teachers of the faith and practitioners helped us to frame every lesson to be age-appropriate and appealing. In addition, a team including respected catechetical, liturgical, pastoral, and theological experts shared their insights and inspired the development of the program.

Contribution to the inspiration and development of the program are:

Dr. Gerard F. Baumbach
Director, Center for Catechetical Initiatives
Concurrent Professor of Theology
University of Notre Dame
Notre Dame, Indiana

Carole M. Eipers, D.Min.
Vice President, Executive Director
    of Catechetics
William H. Sadlier, Inc.

Catechetical and Liturgical Consultants

Reverend Monsignor John F. Barry, P.A.
Pastor, American Martyrs Parish
Manhattan Beach, CA

Patricia Andrews
Director of Religious Education
Our Lady of Lourdes Church,
Slidell, LA

Mary Jo Tully
Chancellor, Archdiocese of Portland

Reverend Monsignor John M. Unger
Deputy Superintendent for Catechesis and
Evangelization
Archdiocese of St. Louis

Curriculum and Child Development Consultants

Brother Robert R. Bimonte, FSC
Executive Director
NCEA Department of Elementary Schools

Sr. Carol Cimino, SSJ, Ed.D.
National Consultant
William H. Sadlier

Gini Shimabukuro, Ed.D.
Associate Professor
Catholic Educational Leadership Program
School of Education
University of San Francisco

Catholic Social Teaching Consultants

John Carr
Executive Director
Department of Justice, Peace,
and Human Development
United States Conference of Catholic Bishops
Washington, D.C.

Joan Rosenhauer
Associate Director
Department of Justice, Peace,
and Human Development
United States Conference of Catholic Bishops
Washington, D.C.

Inculturation Consultants

Allan Figueroa Deck, SJ, Ph.D., S.T.D.
Executive Director, Secretariat of Cultural
Diversity in the Church
United States Conference of Catholic Bishops
Washington, D.C.

Kirk Gaddy, Ed.D.
Educational Consultant
Baltimore, MD

Reverend Nguyễn Việt Hưng
Vietnamese Catechetical Committee

Dulce M. Jiménez-Abreu
Director of Bilingual Programs
William H. Sadlier, Inc.

Contents

UNIT 2

We Are Followers of Jesus 73

SEASONAL CHAPTERS

UNIT 4

We Celebrate and Live Our Faith

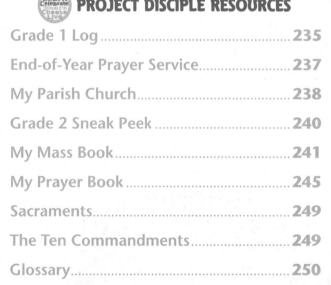

We Believe

The *We Believe* program will help us to

learn

celebrate

share

and live our Catholic faith.

Throughout the year we will hear about many saints and holy people.

Saint Andrew Kim Taegon

Saint Anne

Saint Francis of Assisi

Saint Francis Xavier

Saint John Vianney

Saint Joseph

Saint Katharine Drexel

Saint Patrick

Saints Peter and Paul

Pope Pius X

Saint Teresa of Avila

Blessed Teresa of Calcutta

Together, let us grow as a community of faith.

Welcome!

WE GATHER

✝ **Leader:** Welcome everyone to Grade 1 *We Believe*.

As we begin each chapter, we gather in prayer. We pray to God together.

Let us sing the *We Believe* song!

♫ **We Believe in God**

We believe in God;

We believe, we believe
in Jesus;

We believe in the Spirit
who gives us life.

We believe, we believe
in God.

11

When we see **We Gather** we also come together as a class.

 means it's time to

think about

talk about

write about

draw about

act out

Life

at home

in our neighborhood

at school

in our parish

in our world

Talk about your life right now.

What groups do you belong to?

Why do you like to be a member of these groups?

Each day we learn more about God.

WE BELIEVE

We learn about

- God the Father, God the Son, and God the Holy Spirit

- Jesus, the Son of God, who became one of us

- the Church and its teachings.

We find out about the different ways Catholics live their faith and celebrate God's love.

When we see **We Believe** we learn more about our Catholic faith.

is an open Bible. When we see it, or something like this (John 13:34), we hear the Word of God.

means that we will make the Sign of the Cross and pray.

Key Words means it is time to review the important words we have learned.

means we have an activity. We might

talk   write   act
  draw
       sing
work together   imagine

There are all kinds of activities! We might see  in many parts of our lesson. Be on the lookout!

means it's time to sing! We sing songs we know, make up our own songs, and sing along with those in our *We Believe* music program.

Each of these signs points out something special that we are going to do.

As Catholics...

Here we discover something special about our faith. Don't forget to read it!

WE RESPOND

We can respond by

- thinking about ways our faith affects the things we say and do

- sharing our thoughts and feelings

- praying to God.

Then in our homes, neighborhood, school, parish, and world, we can say and do the things that show love for God and others.

When we see **We Respond** we think about and act on what we have learned about God and our Catholic faith.

In this space, draw yourself as a *We Believe* first grader.

We are so happy you are with us!

Grade 1 Chapter 9

PROJECT

Show What you Know

Match the sentence parts.

The Temple •

Easter Sunday •

• is the special day we celebrate that Jesus Christ rose to new life.

• was the holy place in Jerusalem where the Jewish People prayed.

Celebrate!

Circle the ways you can celebrate that Jesus died and rose for us.

Pray

Praise

Sing

88 www.webelie

DISCIPLE

Picture This What does this stained glass window show?

Jesus is our

_____

Reality Check

The Church teaches us to respect all workers. People work in our neighborhood to protect and care for us. Who helps to protect and care for you?

☐ Police officers
☐ Firefighters
☐ People who keep my neighborhood clean
☐ People in my parish and school

Take Home

What are the two words of praise you learned in this chapter?

_____

_____

Say these words as a family.

89

There are LOADS of ACTIVITIES that make us better disciples! Just look at this additional list.

What's the Word?—all about Scripture

Question Corner—take a quiz

Fast Facts—learn even more about our faith

Make It Happen—living out what we have learned

What Would You Do?—making the right choices

Pray Today—talking and listening to God

Saint Stories—finding great role models

More to Explore—getting information from the Internet and library

Now, Pass It On!—invites us to witness to our faith

Don't forget to look for the **Disciple Challenge**—count how many you can do this year!

And every chapter ends with a Chapter Test!

PROJECT DISCIPLE

You are on a journey this year to become a disciple of Jesus Christ.

Have a great year!

This year you will:

- **learn** the ways God has shown his love for us.

- **pray** at home and with the Church community.

- **celebrate** your faith at Sunday Mass and by honoring the saints.

- **choose** to live as a child of God every day.

- **share** God's gifts with family and others.

- **live out** the Catholic faith by caring for God's creation, especially people.

WE∙BELIEVE

GRADE 1 DISCIPLE CONTRACT

As a disciple of Jesus, this year I promise to

_____

Name

_____

Date

_____

And remember, you can always visit

www.webelieveweb.com

for all kinds of activities, games, study guides, and resources.

Jesus Teaches Us About God's Love

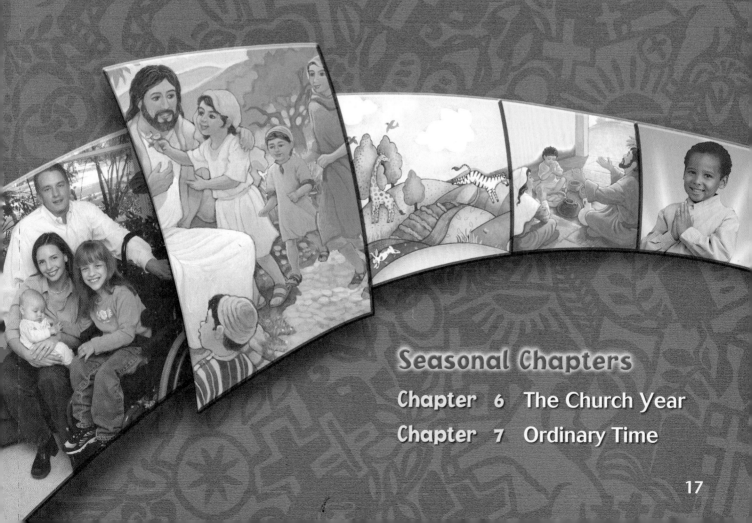

PROJECT DISCIPLE
DEAR FAMILY

In Unit 1 your child will grow as a disciple of Jesus by:

- learning about God the Father's love for all people
- praying to the Blessed Trinity: God the Father, God the Son, and God the Holy Spirit
- meeting Jesus, the Son of God, and the Holy Family
- understanding what Jesus taught us about loving God, ourselves, and others
- living the Great Commandment that Jesus taught.

What Would *you* do?

God wants us to care for all creation. As a family, decide on one way you can do each of the following:

Save water _____

Recycle _____

Add to the beauty of creation _____

Care for animals _____

 **Pray Today** This week, make the Sign of the Cross your special family prayer. You may also want to bless each other at bedtime by tracing a cross on each other's forehead.

Reality Check

"Education in the faith by the parents should begin in the child's earliest years."
(*Catechism of the Catholic Church,* 2226)

Picture This

Together look at the artwork on pages 38 and 39 of the text. Talk about the Holy Family. What are Jesus, Mary, and Joseph doing in the pictures? How did they help each other and show their love for each other? Then talk about the ways your family members help and show love to one another.

What's *the* Word?

Read the Gospel passage from Luke on page 46 in the text. Talk together about the ways God shows he cares for your family. Ask each member to share one way he or she knows God cares. Then offer a prayer of thanks for God's love!

Take Home

Each chapter in your child's *We Believe* Grade 1 text offers a "Take Home" activity that invites your family to support your child's journey to more fully become a disciple of Christ.

Be ready for this unit's Take Home:

Chapter 1: Appreciating God's gifts in the world

Chapter 2: Praying as a family

Chapter 3: Making a family activity collage

Chapter 4: Helping people who are sick

Chapter 5: Learning about people of different cultures

God Is Our Father

WE GATHER

✝ Let us show our thanks to God by singing this song.

🎵 **Thank You, God** *("London Bridge")*

Thank you, God, for Earth, our home.
Earth, our home, Earth, our home.
Thank you, God, for Earth our home.
We say, "Thank you."

(Use the same tune to sing about these gifts in God's world.)

- Thank you, God, for birds and fish.
- Thank you, God, for bugs that crawl.
- Thank you, God, for vegetables.
- Thank you, God, for everything.

☀ Everything in the world is a gift from God. Name your favorite gifts.

WE BELIEVE

God created the world.

The word *create* means "to make."
God created our wonderful world.
Creation is everything God made.

📖 Genesis 1:1–31

Read Along

God created light and water. God created fruits and vegetables. God created all kinds of animals. God created people. Then "God looked at everything he had made, and he found it very good." (Genesis 1:31)

We read about God's creation in the Bible.
The Bible is a special book about God.
The **Bible** is the book of God's Word.
We believe that God is our Father.
We believe that everything he created is good.

Name something beautiful you saw today.
Remember to thank God for this gift.

God created all people.

God wanted to share his love.
So he created people.
We were created to know, love,
and serve God.

God did not create everyone
to be exactly alike.
Every person is special
to God.

God wants people to
take care of his gift
of creation.
He wants us to take
care of his world.

creation everything
God made

Bible the book of
God's Word

Draw a picture to show a way
you can take care of God's world.

God gives us special gifts.

We can do many things that animals and plants cannot do.
We can:

- think and learn
- care for God's world
- share love with our families and friends
- listen to and talk to God.

These things are gifts from God.
God gives us these gifts so we can know and love him.

People are gifts from God, too.
People help us to grow in God's love.

Who are the people who help you to grow in God's love?
Write the first letters of their names on the flower.

As Catholics...

We believe that God created angels. Angels are God's helpers. But they do not have bodies like people do. Angels give people messages from God. They protect and guide us. They never stop praising God.

How can you praise God, too?

God promises to love us always.

God our Father loves us very much.
He wants us to love him.
In the Bible, there is a story about
Adam and Eve.

 Genesis 2–3

Read Along

Adam and Eve lived in the most beautiful garden in the world. Everything was perfect there. God gave them everything they needed to live. God wanted them to be happy with him forever.

One day Adam and Eve did something God told them not to do. Then they had to live in a world that was not perfect anymore.

God never stopped loving Adam and Eve. He promised that he would be with them always. He promised to send someone to help them and their children.

God our Father promises to be
with us and love us always, too.
He promises to save all people.

WE RESPOND

It is important for us to remember
God's promises.
Talk about what God promised us.

Put your right hand over your
heart and pray.
Thank you, God, for loving me always.
I promise to love you in return.

PROJECT

Show What *you* Know

Match the **Key Words** to the pictures.

● **Bible**

● **creation**

Saint Stories

Saint Francis of Assisi loved God. He loved all of God's creation. He took care of God's world. He was kind and gentle to animals. Color this picture of Saint Francis and the animals.

DISCIPLE

Pray
Learn
Celebrate
Share
Choose
Live

Make it Happen

Think about God's gifts of people, plants, and animals. Which of these are you most thankful that God created? Circle your choices.

People

Plants

Animals

Reality Check

Check ways you can take care of God's world.

- ❏ Recycle
- ❏ Love my family
- ❏ Try not to be wasteful
- ❏ Take care of myself

Take Home

Take a walk with your family. Talk about the things you see that God made.

Together say a prayer to thank God for his creation.

CHAPTER TEST

Circle the correct answer.

1. All things made by God are _____.

little   good

2. God created all _____ to know and love him.

people   animals

3. The Bible is a special _____ about God.

book   picture

4. God _____ create everyone to be exactly alike.

did   did not

5. God promises to love us _____.

only at special times   always

 How can people care for all God's creation?

We Believe in the Blessed Trinity

WE GATHER

✝ Let us stand to celebrate God's love.
For each action pray together,
"We thank you, God.
We celebrate your love."

Prayer Actions

- Raise your arms in the air.
- Clap your hands.
- Put your hands over your hearts.
- Close your eyes and bow your heads.

Have you ever waited for something good to happen? How did you feel while you waited?

WE BELIEVE

God sent his own Son, Jesus, to us.

People waited for God to keep his promise to help us.
God the Father had a plan for keeping his promise.
At a special time he sent his own Son to us.
God sent Jesus to live with us on earth.
God sent an angel to ask Mary to be the Mother of his own Son, Jesus.

Jesus showed us

- how much God loves us

- how to love God

- how to love ourselves

- how to love one another.

Jesus promised to help us, too!
He promised to send the Holy Spirit to always be our Helper.

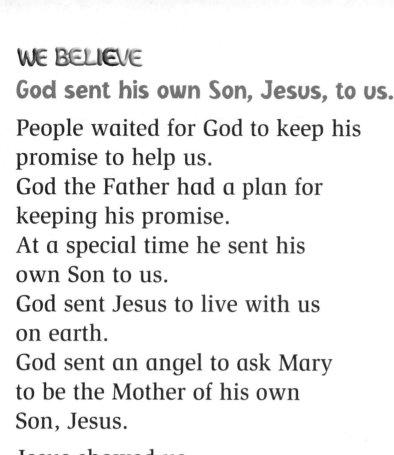 How did God keep his promise to us?

Jesus is God's greatest gift.

Jesus is the Son of God who became one of us.
Jesus is our brother and our friend.

Jesus tells us about God's love.
He tells us that God is our loving Father.
Jesus said, "As the Father loves me, so I also love you." (John 15:9)

Here is a story about Jesus' special love.

Mark 10:13–14

Read Along

One day families came to Jesus with their children. They wanted Jesus to bless the children. Friends of Jesus told these people to go away. But Jesus said, "Let the children come to me." (Mark 10:14)

Draw yourself with Jesus.

There are Three Persons in One God.

Jesus, the Son of God, taught us about God the Father and God the Holy Spirit.

The **Blessed Trinity** is One God in Three Persons.

- God the Father is the First Person of the Blessed Trinity.

- God the Son is the Second Person of the Blessed Trinity.

- God the Holy Spirit is the Third Person of the Blessed Trinity.

God the Father, God the Son, and God the Holy Spirit are joined in love.

Look at the picture of the three circles joined together. Use your favorite color to color the circles. What can this picture help you to remember about the Blessed Trinity?

The Sign of the Cross is a prayer to the Blessed Trinity.

When we pray, we show our love for God. **Prayer** is listening and talking to God. We can pray in our own words. We can say prayers written by others.

We use special actions as we pray the **Sign of the Cross**.

In the name of the Father,

and of the Son,

and of the Holy

Spirit.

Amen.

WE RESPOND

The Sign of the Cross always reminds us that we believe in the Blessed Trinity.

Let us pray the Sign of the Cross now.

Who will you remember when you are making the Sign of the Cross?

PROJECT

Show What *you* Know

Trace the . Talk about each one.

Blessed Trinity

prayer

Sign of the Cross

Picture This

Who is God's greatest gift? Draw him here.

Pray
Learn
Celebrate
Share
Choose
Live

Celebrate!

Draw a line to match the pictures to the words. Then, pray the Sign of the Cross.

In the name of the Father,

Amen.

and of the Holy

Spirit.

and of the Son,

Fast Facts

Catholics begin the Mass by making the Sign of the Cross. This shows they believe in the Blessed Trinity.

Take Home

Prayer is listening to and talking to God. You can pray as a family. Together, say this prayer.

Thank you, God, for the gift of your Son, Jesus.

CHAPTER TEST

Circle the correct answer.

1. Is the Holy Spirit our Helper?

   Yes   **No**

2. Is prayer only talking to God?

   Yes   **No**

3. Did God keep his promise by sending his own Son, Jesus, to us?

   Yes   **No**

4. Is there only one God?

   Yes   **No**

5. Are we praying only to God the Father when we pray the Sign of the Cross?

   Yes   **No**

 Who are the Three Persons of the Blessed Trinity?

Jesus Grew Up in a Family

WE GATHER

 Leader: For our families, that we may all keep growing in God's love, we pray,

All: God, please help us to share your love.

Leader: For families who are going to welcome new babies soon, we pray,

All: God, please help them to grow in your love.

Leader: For families who do not have everything they need to live, we pray,

All: God, please help us to take care of them.

What is special about families?

WE BELIEVE

God chose Mary to be the Mother of his Son.

God loved Mary very much.
Mary always did what God wanted.

 Luke 1:26–35, 38

Read Along

One day God sent an angel to a young girl named Mary. The angel told her not to be afraid. The angel told her that she was going to have a son. Mary was also told to name the child Jesus.

The angel said to Mary, "Therefore the child to be born will be called holy, the Son of God." (Luke 1:35)

Mary told the angel that she would do what God wanted.

Mary is the Mother of God's only Son, Jesus.
Jesus loves his mother.
He wants us to love her, too.

Color the word YES.
Ask Mary to help you say YES to God.

As Catholics...

Each year during the nine days before Christmas, Catholics in Mexico and other countries act out the story of Mary and Joseph on their way to Bethlehem. People take part in this outdoor play called *Las Posadas*. In English these words mean "The Inns." The actors who play Mary and Joseph go from house to house. But no one will let them in until the last day. Then the person playing the innkeeper lets them in. The rest of the people enter and celebrate the birth of Jesus.

How do you celebrate the birth of Jesus with your family?

Jesus was born in Bethlehem.

Mary married a man named Joseph.
Mary was going to have a baby.
Mary and Joseph were waiting for
Jesus to be born.
Joseph would be Jesus' foster father.

Luke 2:1–7

Read Along

During that time a new rule was made. All men
had to go back to the town of their father's family.
They had to sign a list and be counted. Joseph was
from the town of Bethlehem. So he and Mary had
to go there.

When Mary and Joseph got to Bethlehem, it was
very crowded. They looked for a place to stay. There
was no room for them anywhere. At last, they found
a place where animals were kept. They rested there.
Later that night, Mary had a baby boy. "She wrapped
him in swaddling clothes and laid him in a manger,
because there was no room for them in the inn."
(Luke 2:7)

At **Christmas** we celebrate the
birth of God's Son, Jesus.
We can celebrate by sharing the
story of Jesus' birth.

What can you tell your
family and friends about the
birth of Jesus?

Key Word

Christmas the time
when we celebrate
the birth of God's
Son, Jesus

Jesus lived in Nazareth with Mary and Joseph.

We call Jesus, Mary, and Joseph the **Holy Family**.
The Holy Family lived in Nazareth.
Uncles, aunts, and cousins lived there, too.
Jesus and his family loved one another.

Jesus obeyed Mary and Joseph.
He did what they asked him.

What are ways Jesus, Mary, and Joseph helped one another?

Color the heart only if it is next to a way the Holy Family showed their love.

did not share their things

helped each other with chores

were kind to each other

Circle what you will do to help your family.

Key Word

Holy Family the family of Jesus, Mary and Joseph

38

The Holy Family obeyed God the Father and prayed to him.

Jesus, Mary, and Joseph believed
in the one, true God.
They loved God very much.
They obeyed God's laws.

The Holy Family prayed to God.
They prayed every morning
and every night.
They joined other Jewish families
for prayer each week.
They listened to stories
about God and his people.

WE RESPOND

When does your family pray together?
Share this prayer at your family meals.

Bless us, O Lord,
and these your gifts
which we are about to receive
from your goodness.
Through Christ our Lord.
Amen.

PROJECT

Show What you Know

Write the Key Words into the word shapes.

Then, talk about each one.

Christmas

Holy Family

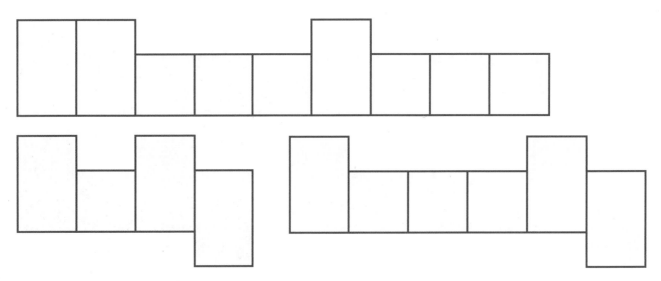

Picture This

Fill in this picture story.

God sent an angel to Mary.

Jesus was born in Bethlehem.

The Holy Family lived in Nazareth.

DISCIPLE

Pray
Learn
Celebrate
Share
Choose
Live

Celebrate!

Complete the chart. Use words or pictures.

What are some ways you celebrate your birthday?	What are some ways you celebrate Jesus' birth?

Reality Check

Check your favorite ways to help your family.

❏ Clean my room

❏ Listen

❏ Be kind

❏ Pray for my family members

_____

❏ _____

(your own way)

Take Home

Gather some family magazines. Find pictures of families doing things together. Make a collage of the different things that *your* family members do together. Talk about ways your family is like the Holy Family.

CHAPTER TEST

Circle the correct answer.

1. Jesus was born in _____.

Bethlehem   Nazareth

2. When Jesus was growing up, the Holy Family lived in _____.

Bethlehem   Nazareth

3. We celebrate the birth of Jesus on _____.

Christmas   Easter

4. Mary _____ did what God asked her to do.

always   never

5. Jesus, Mary, and _____ were members of the Holy Family.

the angel   Joseph

What are some of the things the Holy Family did together?

Jesus Works Among the People

WE GATHER

✝ **Leader:** Jesus is always with us.

🎵 **Jesus in the Morning**

Jesus, Jesus,
Jesus in the morning,
Jesus at the noontime;
Jesus, Jesus,
Jesus when the sun goes down!

Love him, love him,
Love him in the morning,
Love him at the noontime;
Love him, love him,
Love him when the sun goes down!

☀ Have you ever helped someone to welcome a special visitor? What did you do?

WE BELIEVE

John the Baptist helped people to get ready for Jesus.

John was the cousin of Jesus.
When John grew up, he became
one of God's helpers.
John told people to put God first
in their lives.
He told them to share and be fair.

Many people heard John's message.
John, called John the Baptist, was
getting the people ready.
They were getting ready to welcome
Jesus, the Son of God, into their lives.

You need to be ready to welcome
Jesus every day.

Circle one way you can welcome
him today.

Share with my friends.

Say my prayers.

Be fair when I play.

Help my family at home.

Jesus shared God's love with all people.

Jesus went from town to town teaching people.
He told them about God.

Jesus treated all people with respect.
He shared the news of God's love with everyone.
Here is a story about someone Jesus met.

Luke 19:1–5

Read Along

One day Jesus visited a town named Jericho. A large crowd gathered to see Jesus. A very rich man named Zacchaeus wanted to see Jesus, too. Zacchaeus was so short that he could not see above the heads of the other people. He climbed a tree and sat in the branches so that he could see Jesus.

When Jesus came to the tree, he looked up. He said, "Zacchaeus, come down quickly, for today I must stay at your house." (Luke 19:5)

Zacchaeus was very happy.
Jesus was coming to his house.
Jesus knew that Zacchaeus needed to hear the news of God's love.

What did you learn about Jesus from this story?

45

Jesus teaches that God watches over us and cares for us.

 Luke 12:22–24

Read Along

One day Jesus was teaching. He pointed to the birds flying above the crowd. Jesus said that the birds did not have to worry about food. God cares for the birds. Jesus told the crowd that God cares for people even more! He said, "How much more important are you than birds!" (Luke 12:24)

God loves and takes care of us even when we do not know it.
When we believe someone loves us, we **trust** them.
Jesus tells us to trust God.

🎵 People Worry

People worry about this and that.
People worry about this and that!
But Jesus tells us, "Don't worry.
Don't worry about this and that!"

God knows ev'rything we need,
just believe, just believe.
God takes care of ev'ryone.
Trust in God, trust in God.

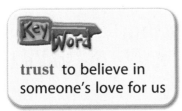

trust to believe in someone's love for us

As Catholics...

We all need to take quiet time to pray to God. We can praise God. We can thank God. We can ask God for help. Before Jesus began to teach, he went into the desert. He went there to pray to God.

Where is your special place to pray?

46

Jesus helped all those in need.

Jesus comforted people who were sad or afraid.
He helped people who were poor or hungry.
He healed people who were sick.

📖 Matthew 20:29-33

Read Along

One day a large crowd was following Jesus. Two blind men heard that Jesus was passing by. They cried out to him for help. Jesus stopped and asked, "What do you want me to do for you?" They answered him, "Lord, let our eyes be opened." (Matthew 20:32–33)

Then Jesus touched their eyes. Right away the two men could see. They began to follow Jesus.

WE RESPOND

What do you think the two men said after Jesus healed them?

🧍 Finish this prayer by matching.

Jesus,

• • Open my ___s. May they *see* people who need help.

• Help my ___s to *hear* your word.

• Let my ___s *do* good for others.

PROJECT

Show What you Know

Write a sentence using the Key Word trust.

_____

- -

_____

What Would you do?

Jess spilled her snack during snack time. She felt sad and hungry. Henry wanted to help Jess.

In the ⬭ write what Henry could say to Jess.

DISCIPLE

Pray
Learn
Celebrate
Share
Choose
Live

Make *it* Happen

Jesus shared the news of God's love with everyone. Draw one way you can share the news of God's love.

Pray Today

Praying for people is another way to help and love them. Think of someone you know who needs your love. Say a prayer for this person.

↳ **DISCIPLE CHALLENGE** Pray your prayer with friends and family.

Take Home ➤

Circle one way your family can share God's love with people who are sick:

- praying for or with them
- cheering them up
- listening to them
- reading Bible stories to them.

- _____
  (another way)

Circle the correct answer.

1. Was Zacchaeus the cousin of Jesus?

Yes   **No**

2. When we trust God, do we believe in his love for us?

Yes   **No**

3. Did Jesus treat all people with respect?

Yes   **No**

4. Did Jesus show God's love by healing the sick?

Yes   **No**

5. Did Jesus stay in Nazareth all his life on earth?

Yes   **No**

 **What did John the Baptist tell people?**

Jesus Teaches Us About Love

WE GATHER

✝ **Leader:** Jesus, you blessed the children who came to see you. We ask you to bless us now.

All: Jesus, bless our eyes so we may see your ♡.

Jesus, bless our ears so we may hear your words of ♡.

Jesus, bless our hands so we may share your ♡.

Jesus, bless our mouths so we may tell others about your ♡.

Jesus, fill our hearts with ♡.

☀ Who do you like to spend time with? Why?

WE BELIEVE

Many people wanted to follow Jesus.

When Jesus taught, crowds of people would come to hear him.

The people needed him to:

- make them feel better
- teach them to pray
- tell them the Good News about God's love
- tell them how to live a better life.

After spending time with Jesus, people came to know what God's love was like.
Jesus made everyone feel special.

How can you spend time with Jesus?
Circle each thing you can do.

- Pray.
- Listen to a story about Jesus.
- Share Jesus' love with others.

Jesus taught the Great Commandment.

Commandments are laws or rules given to us by God.
These laws help us to live as God wants.
Jesus taught us the Great Commandment.

Jesus said,
"You shall love the Lord,
your God, with all your heart,
with all your soul,
and with all your mind.
You shall love your neighbor
as yourself." (Matthew 22:37, 39)

When we follow this commandment, we love God, ourselves, and others.

We show God our love when we

- do what God wants us to do
- pray to God everyday.

Key Word

commandments
laws or rules given to us by God

Write one way you can show your love for God.

_____

_____

Jesus taught us to love God, ourselves, and others.

When we learn about Jesus' teaching, we learn about love. We show God we love ourselves when we take care of ourselves.

Jesus cared for all people. He listened to people's problems. He wants us to act as he acted. We do this when we love God, ourselves, and others.

Color the star beside each picture that shows people acting as Jesus did.

54

Jesus taught us that all people are our neighbors.

After Jesus taught the Great Commandment, someone asked who our neighbors are. Jesus answered by telling this story.

 Luke 10:30–35

Read Along

One day a man was walking down the road. Robbers hurt him and took his money. They left the man on the side of the road. A priest walked by the person who was hurt. He did not stop to help. Then another religious leader passed and saw the hurt man. But he kept walking. Finally, a man from the country called Samaria stopped to help him. He rubbed oil on the man's cuts and covered them with bandages. The Samaritan brought the hurt man to a roadside inn.

The next day the Samaritan had to leave. He said to the innkeeper, "Take care of him. If you spend more than what I have given you, I shall repay you on my way back." (Luke 10:35)

We call the good neighbor the good Samaritan. He cared for and helped the hurt man.

Jesus told this story to help us understand that:

- all people are our neighbors
- we are to be good neighbors to everyone.

WE RESPOND

How will you be a good neighbor in your school or neighborhood this week?

Stand and shake hands with those who are near you.

Pray
Learn
Celebrate
Share
Choose
Live

PROJECT

Show What *you* Know

What are the laws or rules given to us by God?

_____

- -

_____

What Would *you* do?

Follow the path that will bring you closer to Jesus. Use the sign posts to help you.

DISCIPLE

Pray
Learn
Celebrate
Share
Choose
Live

Make it Happen Be a good neighbor. Circle one item from each column and do it today.

Who will you help?	What will you do?
A classmate	Be kind
A family member	Share a story about Jesus
Someone you know in your parish	Teach him or her a prayer

↳ **DISCIPLE CHALLENGE** How are the family members in the picture showing their love for God and one another?

Take Home

Jesus taught us that we are all neighbors. We can show love for our neighbors. With your family, learn more about your neighbors who are from or living in other countries.

CHAPTER TEST

Circle the correct answer.

1. Jesus taught us that _____ people are our neighbors.

all   some

2. _____ people came to hear Jesus.

Many   Few

3. We show God our love when we _____.

hurt others   love ourselves

4. Commandments are _____ given to us by God.

laws   tests

5. Jesus _____ people's problems.

forgot about   listened to

 **TALK ABOUT IT** What did Jesus teach us in the story of the good Samaritan?

Praise to you, Lord Jesus Christ.

SEASONAL

CHAPTER 6

This chapter presents an overview of the Church Year.

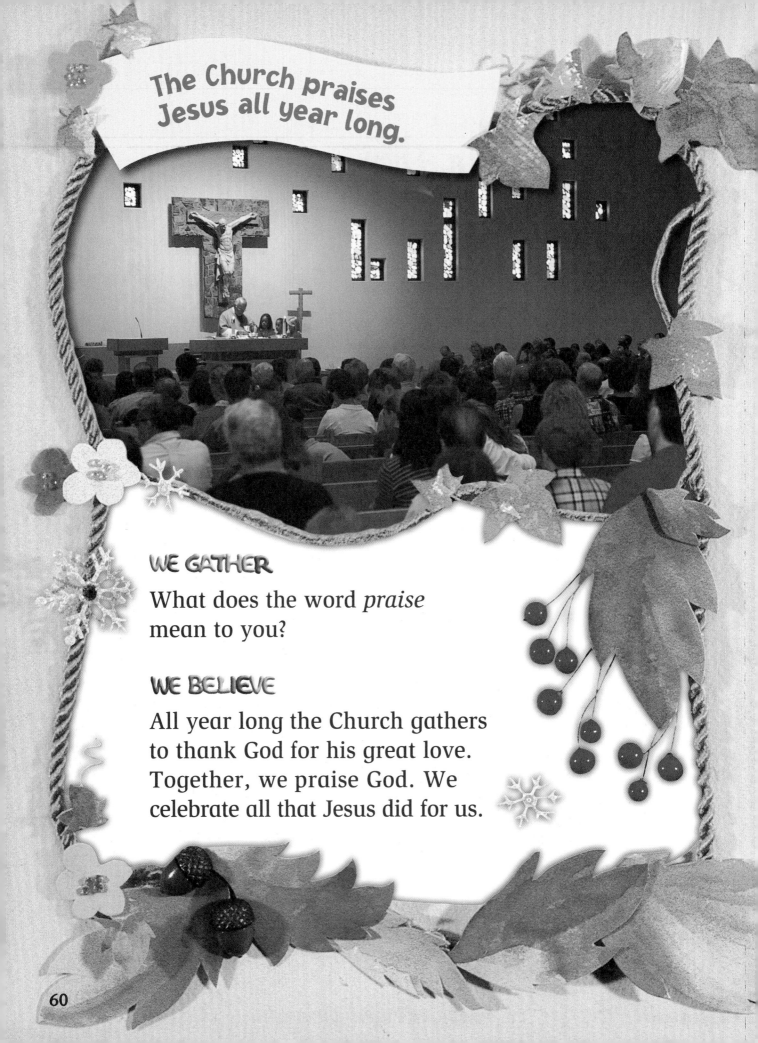

The Church praises Jesus all year long.

WE GATHER

What does the word *praise* mean to you?

WE BELIEVE

All year long the Church gathers to thank God for his great love. Together, we praise God. We celebrate all that Jesus did for us.

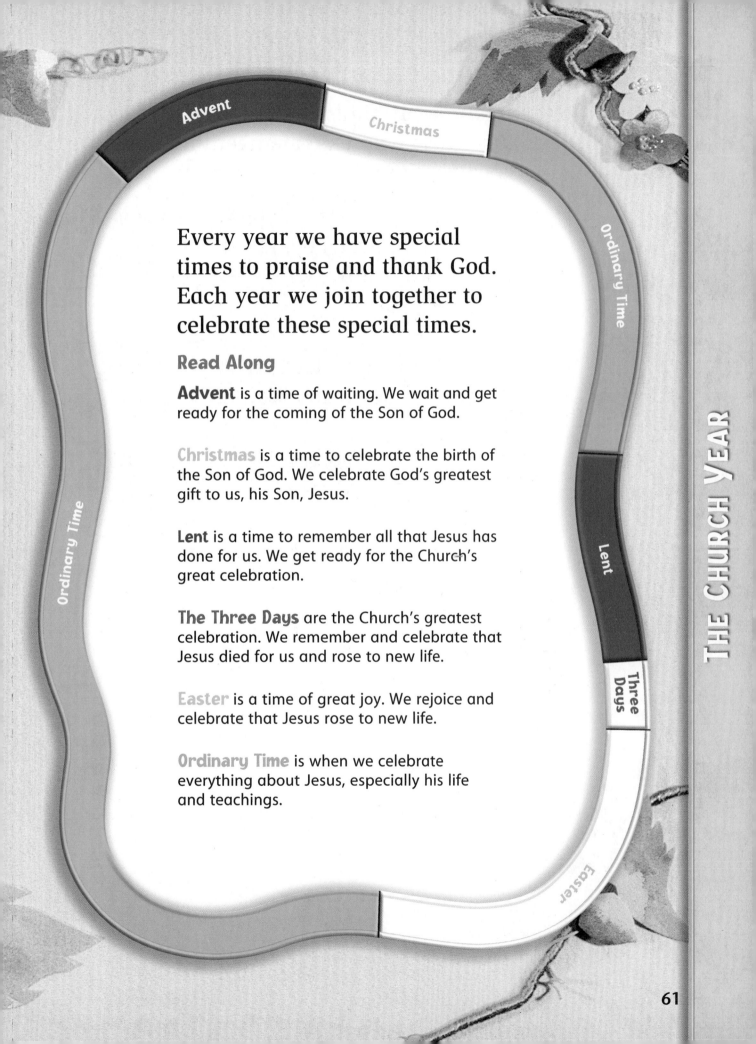

Every year we have special times to praise and thank God. Each year we join together to celebrate these special times.

Read Along

Advent is a time of waiting. We wait and get ready for the coming of the Son of God.

Christmas is a time to celebrate the birth of the Son of God. We celebrate God's greatest gift to us, his Son, Jesus.

Lent is a time to remember all that Jesus has done for us. We get ready for the Church's great celebration.

The Three Days are the Church's greatest celebration. We remember and celebrate that Jesus died for us and rose to new life.

Easter is a time of great joy. We rejoice and celebrate that Jesus rose to new life.

Ordinary Time is when we celebrate everything about Jesus, especially his life and teachings.

Advent

Christmas

Ordinary Time

Ordinary Time

Lent

Three Days

Easter

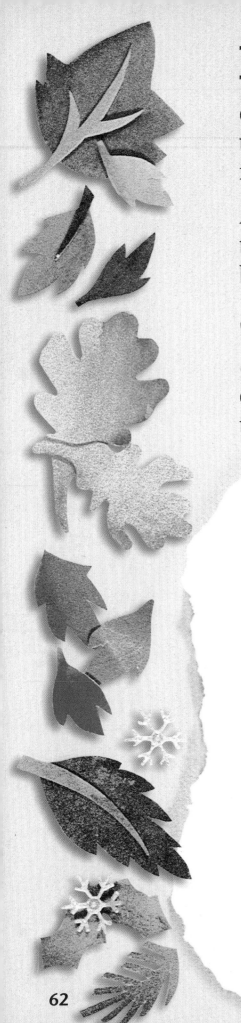

The Church year helps us to follow Jesus. The different times help us remember and celebrate all that Jesus did for us. The times also help us remember that Jesus is with us today!

All during the year we thank Jesus for the gift of himself. We thank him for being with us always.

WE RESPOND

In the empty space, draw something or someone for whom you are thankful to Jesus.

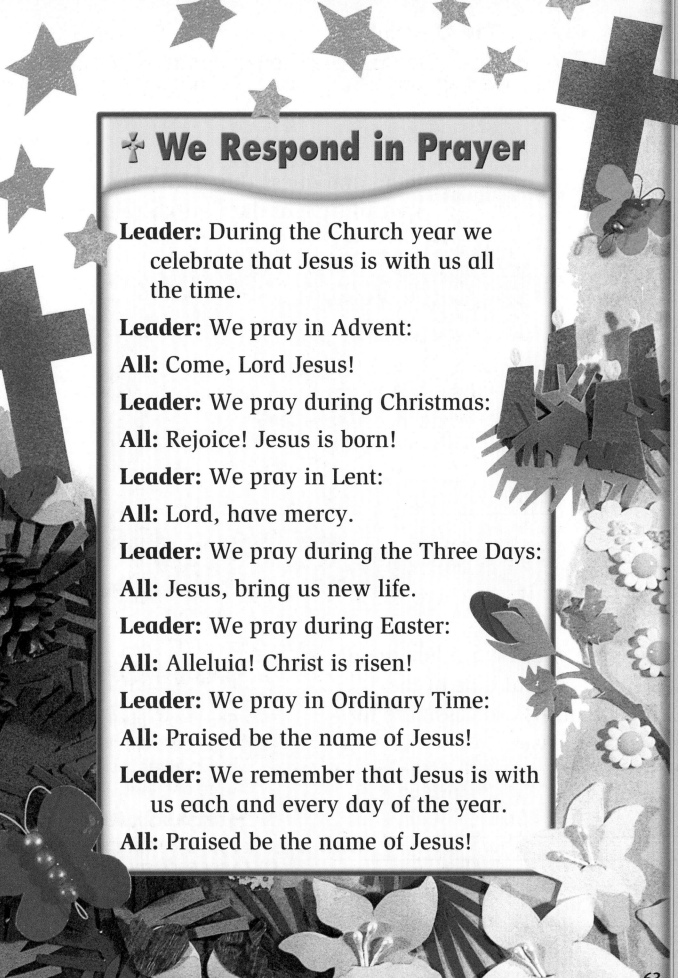

✝ We Respond in Prayer

Leader: During the Church year we celebrate that Jesus is with us all the time.

Leader: We pray in Advent:

All: Come, Lord Jesus!

Leader: We pray during Christmas:

All: Rejoice! Jesus is born!

Leader: We pray in Lent:

All: Lord, have mercy.

Leader: We pray during the Three Days:

All: Jesus, bring us new life.

Leader: We pray during Easter:

All: Alleluia! Christ is risen!

Leader: We pray in Ordinary Time:

All: Praised be the name of Jesus!

Leader: We remember that Jesus is with us each and every day of the year.

All: Praised be the name of Jesus!

Celebrate!

Read and guess this riddle about a special time of the Church year.

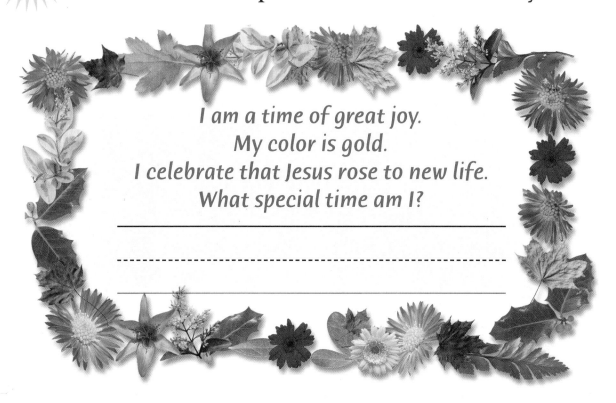

I am a time of great joy.
My color is gold.
I celebrate that Jesus rose to new life.
What special time am I?

_____

_____

Now, write your own riddle about a different special time of the Church year. Ask a classmate to guess the answer.

_____

_____

_____

_____

Take Home

See if your family members can guess the riddle you have written. Ask them to write one too!

↳ **DISCIPLE CHALLENGE** With your family, write riddles for each special time of the Church year.

Give thanks to the Lord,
his love is everlasting.

SEASONAL

This chapter helps us to understand
the season of Ordinary Time.

CHAPTER 7

The Church celebrates the life and teachings of Jesus.

WE GATHER

We can put things in order by numbering them.

What is the biggest number of things that you have put in order?

WE BELIEVE

The Church has special times to celebrate. During Ordinary Time, we celebrate the life and teachings of Jesus. We try to follow him more closely each day. This season is called Ordinary Time because the Church puts the Sundays in number *order*.

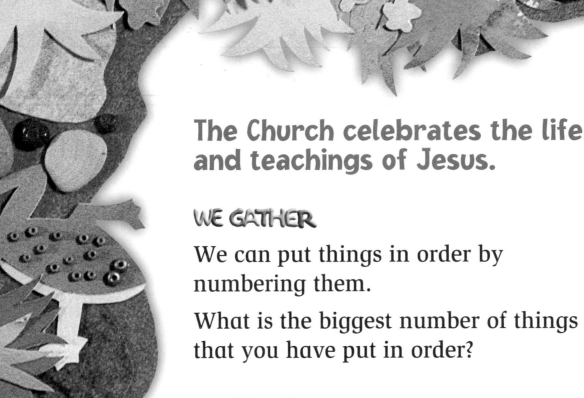

Every Sunday of the year is a special day. Every Sunday we celebrate the Mass. We remember the things Jesus has done for us. We thank Jesus for the gift of himself.

We hear wonderful
stories about

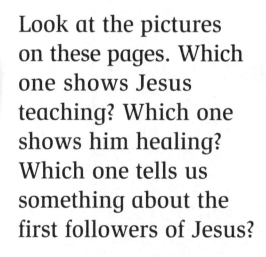

- Jesus' teaching, healing, and forgiving
- the first followers of Jesus
- the Holy Spirit helping the first members of the Church.

Look at the pictures on these pages. Which one shows Jesus teaching? Which one shows him healing? Which one tells us something about the first followers of Jesus?

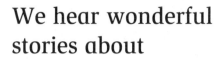 Share your answers.

Saints are followers of Jesus who loved him very much. The saints have died, but they now live forever with God. The lives of the saints show us how to be followers of Jesus.

We celebrate many special days during Ordinary Time. One of them is called All Saints' Day. It is celebrated on November 1.

WE RESPOND

Draw yourself here. Write one way you are a follower of Jesus.

✝ We Respond in Prayer

Leader: We are all children of God. On All Saints' Day, we celebrate all the children of God who are living forever with God. They are called saints.

Reader: Let us listen to the Word of God.

"Blessed are the peacemakers,
for they will be called children
of God." (Matthew 5:9)

The Gospel of the Lord.

All: Praise to you, Lord Jesus Christ.

Leader: The saints are children of God. We honor them because they loved God and loved others. We are children of God. We can love God and love others, too!

🎵 Children of God

Children of God is what we are.
Children of God we all must be.
Children of God; that's you and me.
Thanks be to God.
Thanks be to God.
We all stand in need to be thankful
for making us children of God.

PROJECT DISCIPLE

Celebrate!

Trace this special message!
Decorate the banner.

I am a child
of God.

What's *the* Word?

Jesus said, "Love one another as I love you" (John 15:12).

Check the ways Jesus showed his love.

- ❏ Teaching
- ❏ Healing
- ❏ Forgiving
- ❏ Helping

Take Home

As a family, talk about ways you follow Jesus everyday. Write them below.

Everyday, we follow Jesus by

_____

_____

Fill in the circle beside the correct answer.

1. The Bible is a special book about _____.

○ God   ○ trees

2. God sent his own Son, _____, to us.

○ Joseph   ○ Jesus

3. On Christmas, we celebrate the birth of _____.

○ Jesus   ○ Joseph

4. Jesus taught us that we should be good neighbors to _____.

○ everyone   ○ people we know

Circle the correct answer.

5. Was Jesus mean to people?   **Yes   No**

6. Did God create the world?   **Yes   No**

7. Did Jesus teach us that God watches
over us and cares for us?   **Yes   No**

8. Was Zacchaeus Jesus' only follower?   **Yes   No**

continued on next page

Look at the two pictures below.
For each picture, write what Jesus is doing
and saying.

9.

_____
- -
_____
_____
_____
- -
_____

10.

_____
- -
_____
_____
- -
_____
- -
_____

We Are Followers of Jesus

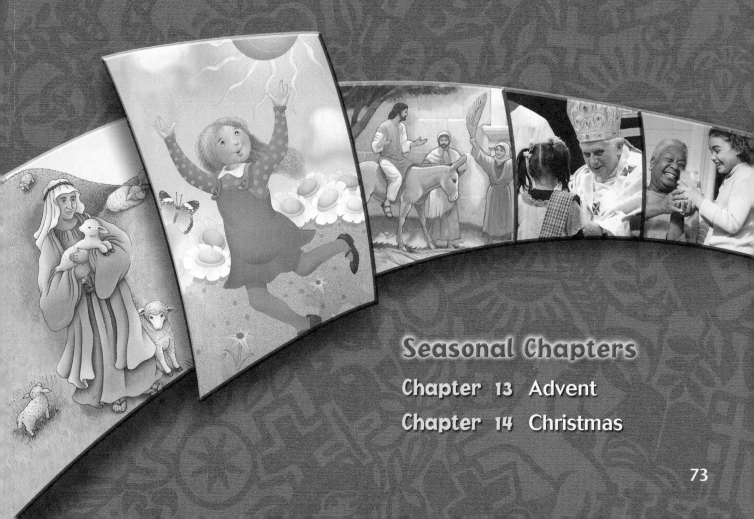

Seasonal Chapters

Pray
Learn
Celebrate
Share
Choose
Live

PROJECT DISCIPLE
DEAR FAMILY

In Unit 2 your child will grow as a disciple of Jesus by:

- appreciating that Jesus had many followers, and he taught them to pray
- understanding that Jesus died and rose to bring us new life
- learning that Jesus Christ sent the Holy Spirit to his followers
- hearing the story of Pentecost, and the ways the Holy Spirit helps the Church to grow
- recognizing that the pope and bishops lead the Church in caring for and serving others.

Celebrate!

This image is a model of the Temple in Jerusalem during Jesus' time. Jesus was Jewish, and so the roots of our Catholic faith are Jewish. If you have Jewish friends, invite them for a meal and celebrate your common heritage. Pray for all Jewish People.

Show That You Care

In Chapter 12 your child will learn about the pope and the bishops. Help your child to name the Church leaders. (Visit your parish Web site.)

Our pope is _____

Our bishop is _____

Our pastor is _____

Our parish ministers are _____

Together thank God for those who serve the Church today.

Reality Check

"Parents' respect and affection are expressed by the care and attention they devote to bringing up their young children and *providing for their physical and spiritual needs*."

(*Catechism of the Catholic Church*, 2228)

Pray Today

Pray the Lord's Prayer together. Talk about the ways your family can help the Kingdom of God to grow. Remind your child that you always pray the Lord's Prayer at Mass on Sunday.

Fast Facts

The Church uses several symbols to represent the Holy Spirit: a flame, a dove, clouds and light, a hand, and others. In your church, look for any symbols for the Holy Spirit. Which symbol means the most to your family?

Take Home

Each chapter in your child's *We Believe* Grade 1 text offers a "Take Home" activity that invites your family to support your child's journey to more fully become a disciple of Christ.

Be ready for this unit's Take Home:

Chapter 8: Praying the Lord's Prayer together

Chapter 9: Praising God

Chapter 10: Joining the parish for breakfast

Chapter 11: Making a Holy Spirit poster

Chapter 12: Pledging to serve others

Jesus Had Many Followers

WE GATHER

✝ Let us pray by singing.

🎵 **Jesus Wants to Help Us**

We believe Jesus wants to help us.
We believe Jesus wants to help us.
We believe that Jesus
   always wants to help us.

When we pray, Jesus wants to hear us.
When we pray, Jesus wants to hear us.
We believe that Jesus
   always wants to hear us.

☀ How do you feel when
you get a special invitation
from a friend?

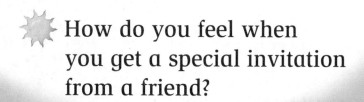

WE BELIEVE

Jesus invited people to be his followers.

Jesus invited people to come and be with him.
He asked people to be his followers.

 Matthew 4:18–20

Read Along

One day Jesus was walking by the sea. He saw two brothers fishing. Their names were Peter and Andrew. Jesus invited Peter and Andrew to be his followers. "At once they left their nets and followed him." (Matthew 4:20)

Jesus asked other men and women to be his followers, too.
Jesus' followers learned from him.
They tried to act as Jesus did.
They shared God's love with others, too.

Jesus had many followers.
The **Apostles** were the twelve men Jesus chose to lead his followers.

Jesus invites you to be his follower, too.
If you want to be a follower of Jesus, write your name here.

_____

- -

_____

Key Word

Apostles the twelve men Jesus chose to lead his followers

Jesus' followers believed that he was the Son of God.

Jesus spent a lot of time with his followers.
They trusted Jesus very much.

Here is a story about a time when Jesus helped his followers.

Luke 8:22–25

Read Along

One day Jesus was in a boat with his followers. He fell asleep. Soon a storm started rocking the boat. Jesus' followers were afraid. They woke Jesus up. They believed he would help them.

Jesus told the winds and waves to be still. Jesus' followers were amazed because the storm stopped. They asked, "Who then is this, who commands even the winds and the sea, and they obey him?" (Luke 8:25)

Jesus did amazing things to help people.
He did many things that only God can do.
Jesus' followers saw these things and believed in him.
They believed Jesus was the Son of God.

Act out what you would have said to Jesus after he calmed the storm.

Jesus showed his followers how to pray.

Jesus often prayed to God the Father.
Sometimes Jesus prayed alone.
Sometimes he prayed with other people.

Jesus' followers learned to pray by watching him pray.
They learned to pray by listening to Jesus, too.

 Luke 11:1–2

Read Along

One day Jesus was praying. When he was finished, one of his followers asked him to teach the group to pray. Jesus told his followers, "When you pray, say: 'Father, hallowed be your name.'" (Luke 11:2)

We call the prayer Jesus taught his followers the **Lord's Prayer**.

We also call this prayer the Our Father.

Why do you pray?
Who teaches you to pray?
Write two names here.

Lord's Prayer the prayer Jesus taught his followers

_____

_____

Thank these people and say a prayer for them.

We pray the Lord's Prayer.

We can pray the Lord's Prayer
with others or by ourselves.
Here are the words we pray.

The Lord's Prayer

Our Father, who art in heaven,
hallowed be thy name;
thy kingdom come;
thy will be done on earth as it is
   in heaven.
Give us this day our daily bread;
and forgive us our trespasses
as we forgive those who trespass
   against us;
and lead us not into temptation,
but deliver us from evil.
Amen.

WE RESPOND

Gather in a circle.
Pray the Lord's Prayer
together.

As Catholics...

Lord is another name for God.
Jesus' followers sometimes called
him Lord. We use the name *Lord* in
many of our prayers. When we do
this, we remember that Jesus is the
Son of God. During Sunday Mass,
listen for the times we pray, "Lord."

Pray
Learn
Celebrate
Share
Choose
Live

Show What *you* Know

Apostles

Lord's Prayer

Write the  that answers each question.

What is the prayer Jesus taught his followers?

_____

- -

_____

Who are the twelve men Jesus chose to lead his followers?

_____

- -

_____

Pray Today

Many fishermen in France pray this prayer. It shows they trust God.

Dear God,
be good to me.
The sea is so wide,
and my boat is so small.
(Fishers of Brittany, France)

DISCIPLE

Pray
Learn
Celebrate
Share
Choose
Live

What's *the* Word?

Jesus taught us to pray the Lord's Prayer. Part of this prayer is, "Give us this day our daily bread." When we pray these words, we are praying for the needs of all people. Draw some things that people need today.

Make *it* Happen

Finish this message to Jesus. As your friend and follower, I can

❏ share my toys.

❏ pay attention in school.

❏ say my prayers.

❏ help a friend.

_____

- -

❏ _____
(your own way)

Take Home

Share the stories about Jesus you have learned this week. Pray the Lord's Prayer together as a family. Talk about what the words mean.

Circle the correct answer.

1. The _____ of Jesus learned from him.

teachers   followers

2. Jesus' followers believed that he was _____.

the Son of God   an Apostle

3. Jesus taught his followers the _____.

Sign of the Cross   Lord's Prayer

4. The _____ men Jesus chose to lead his followers were the Apostles.

twelve   ten

5. Jesus _____ prayed to God the Father.

never   often

What did Jesus do to help his followers in the storm?

WE GATHER

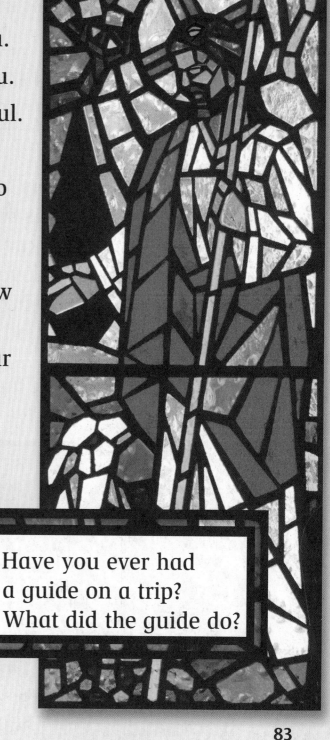

✝ **Leader:** Jesus, today we gather together to pray to you.

All: Jesus, we believe in you.

Leader: Jesus, you are wonderful.

All: Jesus, we praise you.

Leader: Jesus, you have done so much for us.

All: Jesus, we thank you.

Leader: Jesus, we want to follow you.

All: Jesus, help us to be your followers.

Have you ever had a guide on a trip? What did the guide do?

WE BELIEVE

Jesus told his followers that he loved and cared for them.

Jesus wanted his followers to understand what he was teaching. He talked about things they knew about.

 John 10:2, 14

Read Along

One day Jesus was talking about shepherds. He said, "I am the good shepherd, and I know mine and mine know me." (John 10:14)

Jesus is our Good Shepherd.
He is with us always.
He knows each one of us.
He loves us very much.
He shows us ways to love God and others.

Trace the path that shows ways to love God and others.

What signs did you follow along the way?

84

Many people gathered to welcome and praise Jesus.

Jesus visited many towns.
People welcomed him in different ways.
Some began to believe that Jesus
was sent by God.

John 12:12–13

Read Along

Many people were in Jerusalem for a feast. They heard that Jesus was near the city, so they ran out to meet him. They waved palm branches in the air. They shouted, "Hosanna!" (John 12:13)

Hosanna is a word of praise.
The people that day were happy
to see Jesus.
They shouted Hosanna to praise him.
They waved palm branches, too.

Show some ways we can praise Jesus.

As Catholics...

During every Mass we pray Hosanna. We pray the same words the people did when they welcomed Jesus to Jerusalem. We show that we believe Jesus is the Son of God. At Mass next week, praise Jesus for all he has done for us.

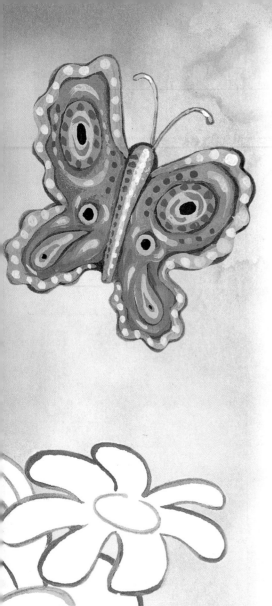

Jesus taught in the Temple in Jerusalem.

Jerusalem is an important city to Jews.
They go there for special feasts.
They go there to pray.

Jerusalem was very important in Jesus' time, too.
Jesus went to Jerusalem.
He taught in the Temple there.

The **Temple** was the holy place in Jerusalem where the Jewish People prayed.

 Luke 21:37–38

Read Along

During the week before Jesus died, he taught in the Temple area every day. "And all the people would get up early each morning to listen to him." (Luke 21:38)

🎵 In the House of Our God

In the House of our God,
In the House of our God,
We give praise to the Lord
In the House of our God.

🏃 Talk about where you go to pray and listen to Jesus' teachings.

Jesus died and rose.

Jesus cared for people.
He shared God's love with them.
Jesus showed his love in a special way.

Jesus died so that all people could live in God's love.
After he died his body was placed in a tomb.
On the third day after Jesus died, something wonderful happened.

 Matthew 28:1–7

Read Along

Early on Sunday morning, some women went to visit Jesus' tomb. They saw an angel sitting in front of the tomb. The angel said, "Do not be afraid!" (Matthew 28:5)

The angel told the women that Jesus had risen to new life. He told them to go tell the other followers.

Jesus died and rose to bring us new life.
Easter Sunday is the special day we celebrate that Jesus Christ rose to new life.

We pray Alleluia, a word of praise.

WE RESPOND

How does your family celebrate Easter Sunday?

Celebrate what Jesus did for us.
Color the Alleluia garden.

Temple the holy place in Jerusalem where the Jewish People prayed

Easter Sunday the special day we celebrate that Jesus Christ rose to new life

Alleluia

Alleluia

Pray Learn Celebrate Share Choose Live

PROJECT

Show What *you* Know

Match the sentence parts.

The Temple ●   ● is the special day we celebrate that Jesus Christ rose to new life.

Easter Sunday ●   ● was the holy place in Jerusalem where the Jewish People prayed.

Celebrate!

Circle the ways you can celebrate that Jesus died and rose for us.

Pray

Praise

Sing

DISCIPLE

Pray
Learn
Celebrate
Share
Choose
Live

Picture This

What does this stained glass window show?

Jesus is our

_____

- -

_____

Reality Check

The Church teaches us to respect all workers. People work in our neighborhood to protect and care for us. Who helps to protect and care for you?

❏ Police officers

❏ Firefighters

❏ People who keep my neighborhood clean

❏ People in my parish and school

Take Home

What are the two words of praise you learned in this chapter?

_____

_____

Say these words as a family.

89

CHAPTER TEST

Circle the correct answer.

1. The word people used to praise Jesus as he entered Jerusalem was _____.

   Hosanna   Alleluia

2. The _____ was the holy place in Jerusalem where the Jewish People prayed.

   Mountain   Temple

3. _____ died and rose to bring us new life.

   Jesus   Peter

4. _____ is the special day we celebrate that Jesus Christ rose to new life.

   Easter Sunday   Christmas Day

5. The city of Jerusalem was _____ in the time of Jesus.

   not important   very important

 Why did Jesus call himself the Good Shepherd?

WE GATHER

✝ **Leader:** Let us celebrate that Jesus Christ rose to new life on Easter.

🎵 **Sing for Joy**

Sing and shout for joy, alleluia!
Sing and shout for joy, alleluia!
Sing and shout for joy, alleluia!
Alleluia! Alleluia!

Leader: Jesus wanted his followers to know that they would not be alone.

 Luke 24:36, 49

Read Along

Jesus did not want his followers to be afraid. He said to them, "Peace be with you." (Luke 24:36) Jesus promised his followers that he would send them a helper.

All: Jesus, thank you for sharing your peace and love.

☀ Have you ever been surprised? What happened?

Alleluia!

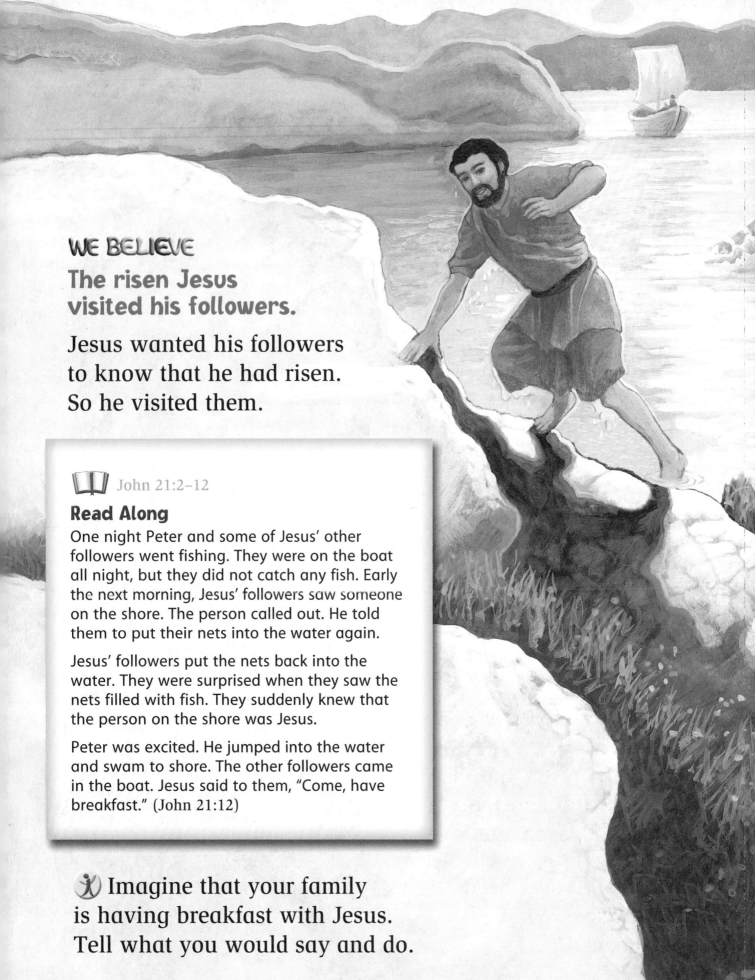

WE BELIEVE

The risen Jesus visited his followers.

Jesus wanted his followers to know that he had risen. So he visited them.

John 21:2–12

Read Along

One night Peter and some of Jesus' other followers went fishing. They were on the boat all night, but they did not catch any fish. Early the next morning, Jesus' followers saw someone on the shore. The person called out. He told them to put their nets into the water again.

Jesus' followers put the nets back into the water. They were surprised when they saw the nets filled with fish. They suddenly knew that the person on the shore was Jesus.

Peter was excited. He jumped into the water and swam to shore. The other followers came in the boat. Jesus said to them, "Come, have breakfast." (John 21:12)

Imagine that your family is having breakfast with Jesus. Tell what you would say and do.

Jesus Christ promised that the Holy Spirit would come to his followers.

The risen Christ was going to return to the Father in Heaven. Jesus wanted his followers to remember him.
He wanted them to tell others about God's love.
He promised that the Holy Spirit would come to be with them.

The Holy Spirit would help Jesus' followers to:

- remember the things Jesus had said and done

- love others as Jesus had taught them

- tell others about Jesus.

After he made this promise, Jesus returned to his Father.

🧍 Write one thing you want to tell someone about Jesus.

_____

_____

Who will you tell this to today?

The Holy Spirit was sent to Jesus' followers.

After Jesus returned to Heaven, his followers went to Jerusalem. They prayed and waited for the Holy Spirit there.

 Acts of the Apostles 2:1–4

Read Along

Early one morning, Jesus' followers were together in one place. Jesus' mother, Mary, was with them. Suddenly, they heard a sound like a strong wind. Then they saw what looked like flames of fire over each of them. "And they were all filled with the holy Spirit." (Acts of the Apostles 2:4)

Pentecost is the day the Holy Spirit came to Jesus' followers.
We celebrate Pentecost fifty days after Easter Sunday.
On this day we celebrate the coming of the Holy Spirit.
Every day we remember that the Holy Spirit is with us.

How do you think Jesus' followers felt on Pentecost?

As Catholics...

The Holy Spirit helps us to share God's love with others. God's love brings light and warmth to the world. This is why the Church often uses a picture of a flame or fire to remind us of the Holy Spirit. Fire gives us light and warmth.

Remember to pray to the Holy Spirit often.

The Holy Spirit is the Third Person of the Blessed Trinity.

The Holy Spirit is always with us. The Blessed Trinity is One God in Three Persons. God the Holy Spirit is the Third Person of the Blessed Trinity.

Here is a prayer we say to praise the Blessed Trinity.

Pentecost the day the Holy Spirit came to Jesus' followers

Glory to the Father,
and to the Son,
and to the Holy Spirit:
as it was in the beginning,
is now, and will be forever.
Amen.

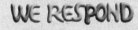

WE RESPOND

Decorate the prayer frame. Together think of actions to use when you pray these words of praise.

Pray this prayer together now with the actions.

95

 Pray Learn Celebrate Share Choose Live

PROJECT

Show What you Know

Use the word shape to write the 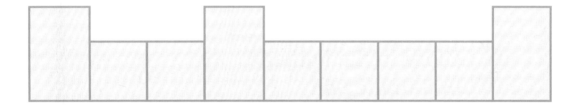 Key Word.
It is the day the Holy Spirit came to
Jesus' followers.

Pentecost

Reality Check

What can the Holy Spirit help
you to do today?

❏ Remember the things Jesus
said and did

❏ Love others as Jesus taught

❏ Tell others about Jesus

❏ Tell others about God's love

DISCIPLE

Pray
Learn
Celebrate
Share
Choose
Live

Picture This

Draw a flame of fire over each of Jesus' followers to remind you that the Holy Spirit came upon them.

Make it Happen

Name a prayer to the Blessed Trinity.

↳ **DISCIPLE CHALLENGE**

Say it.

Teach it to your friend.

Take Home

In many parishes, people join one another for breakfast after Sunday Mass. They talk with people they know. They meet new people. Check your parish bulletin or Web site to see if your parish does this. If so, plan to join in as a family.

Circle the correct answer.

1. Did Jesus visit his followers after he rose from the dead?

Yes   No

2. Did Jesus promise that the Holy Spirit would come to his followers?

Yes   No

3. Was Christmas the day the Holy Spirit came to Jesus' followers?

Yes   No

4. Is the Holy Spirit the Third Person of the Blessed Trinity?

Yes   No

5. Did Jesus want his followers to forget him?

Yes   No

 What did the Holy Spirit help Jesus' followers to do?

The Holy Spirit Helps the Church to Grow

11

WE GATHER

✝ **Leader:** Holy Spirit, we know you are with us all the time. When we are excited or happy,

All: Holy Spirit, fill our  with love.

Leader: When we are sad or lonely,

All: Holy Spirit, fill our  with love.

Leader: When we feel strong or brave,

All: Holy Spirit, fill our  with love.

Leader: When we are tired or afraid,

All: Holy Spirit, fill our  with love.

☀ Think about something exciting that happened to you. Who did you tell about it?

WE BELIEVE

The Church began on Pentecost.

On Pentecost Jesus' followers were excited.
The Holy Spirit had come to them.
They wanted to tell people what
had happened.

Acts of the Apostles 2:36–38, 41

Read Along

On Pentecost, Peter and the other Apostles told people
about Jesus. Peter told the people to believe in Jesus.
He asked them to become Jesus' followers. If they did
this, they would receive the Holy Spirit.

That day about three thousand people received the Gift
of the Holy Spirit. They became followers of Jesus.

This was the beginning of the Church.
The **Church** is all the people who believe
in Jesus and follow his teachings.

Add yourself to the picture.
Pretend you are in the crowd.
Tell what you are seeing and hearing.

The first members of the Church did many things together.

The first members of the Church were like a close family.
They talked about Jesus' teachings.
They learned together about ways to follow Jesus.
They shared the things they had.
They praised God together.

🎵 The First Church Members

("Here We Go 'Round the Mulberry Bush")

The first Church members
   shared their things,
shared their things,
   shared their things.
The first Church members
   shared their things,
and we can do the same.

Sing this song again using these words:
The first Church members
   prayed together.

🏃 How can you live like the first Church members lived?

Key Word

Church all the people who believe in Jesus and follow his teachings

101

The Holy Spirit helped the Church to grow.

The first members of the Church were filled with the Holy Spirit.

With the help of the Holy Spirit, they:

- believed in Jesus
- told everyone what Jesus had done for them
- shared God's love with others
- helped those who were poor or sick
- tried to be kind and fair to everyone.

Every day more and more people became members of the Church.

Circle every other letter. Use the letters in the circles to find the missing word.

Q G A R M O S W

The Holy Spirit helps the Church to

_____ _____ _____ _____ .

The Holy Spirit helps the Church today.

The Holy Spirit is always with the Church. We are members of the Church. The Holy Spirit helps us to know that Jesus loves us. The Holy Spirit helps us to live as Jesus taught us.

With the help of the Holy Spirit we:

- pray
- share with others
- care for those who are poor or sick
- show respect for all people
- learn more about Jesus and the Church.

WE RESPOND

What can you and your family do to live as Jesus taught us?

🎵 Share the Light

Share the light of Jesus.
Share the light that shows the way.
Share the light of Jesus.
Share God's spirit today.
Share God's spirit today.

As Catholics...

After the Church began, Paul became a member, too. Like Peter, he told everyone he met about Jesus. Paul taught that all people were welcome in the Church.

On June 29, the Church honors Saint Peter and Saint Paul. On this day, we remember that Peter and Paul helped the Church to grow. You can learn more about Saint Peter and Saint Paul in the Bible.

PROJECT

Show What *you* Know

Trace the **Key Word** in every faith statement.
Think about what it means.

The Church began on Pentecost.

The first members of the Church did many things together.

The Holy Spirit helped the Church to grow.

The Holy Spirit helps the Church today.

Fast Facts

Here are some ways to thank members of the Church all over the world.

thank you	English
kam sa ham ni da	Korean
dziekuje	Polish
gracias	Spanish
ahsante	Swahili
malo malo	Tongan

Pray
Learn
Celebrate
Share
Choose
Live

Reality Check

How are your family members like the first Church members?

- ❑ We talk about Jesus' teachings.
- ❑ We learn about ways to follow Jesus.
- ❑ We share our money.

- ❑ We share our things.
- ❑ We eat together.
- ❑ We praise God together.

Make it Happen

Make up prayer actions to the "Share the Light" song you learned. Then, teach it to your friend.

Now, pass it on!

Take Home

Make a poster with your family to show how the Holy Spirit is with the Church today. Use pictures from a magazine or draw your own. Write words to go with your pictures.

Circle the correct answer.

1. The Church began on _____.

   Pentecost   Easter

2. The first members of the Church _____.

   did not share   shared many things

3. The _____ is all the people who believe in Jesus and follow his teachings.

   Holy Spirit   Church

4. The Holy Spirit helps us to live as _____ taught us.

   the crowd   Jesus

5. The first members of the Church were _____ the Holy Spirit.

   filled with   tired of

 What does the Holy Spirit help us to do?

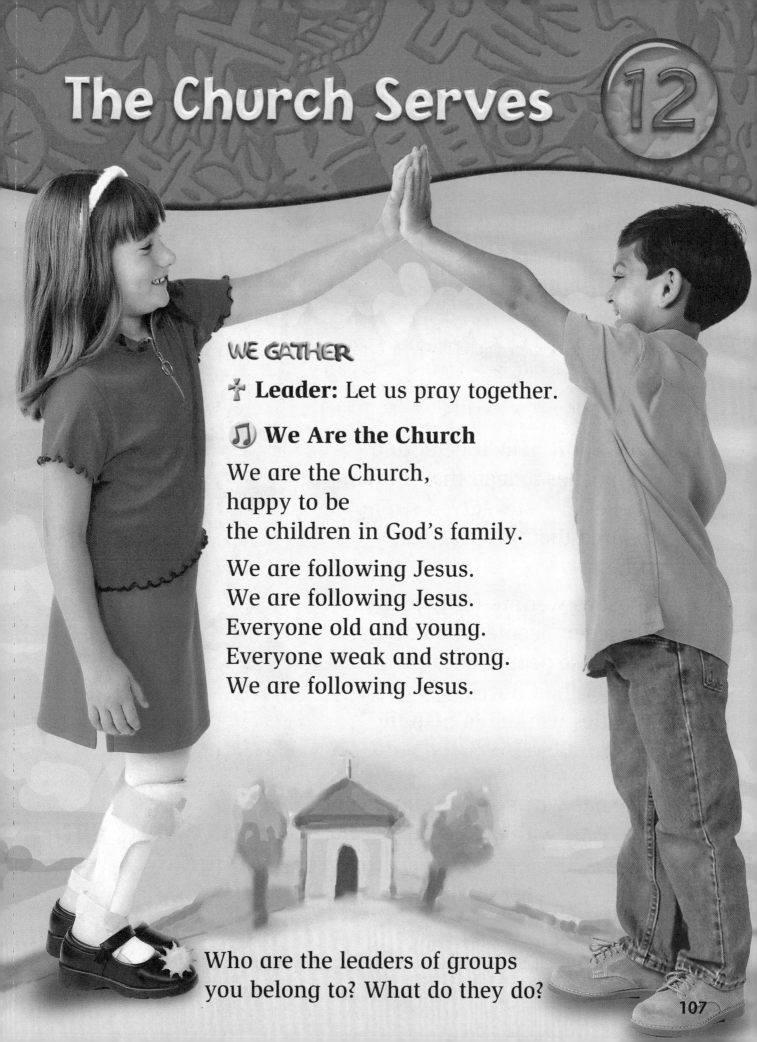

The Church Serves

12

WE GATHER

✝ **Leader:** Let us pray together.

🎵 **We Are the Church**

We are the Church,
happy to be
the children in God's family.

We are following Jesus.
We are following Jesus.
Everyone old and young.
Everyone weak and strong.
We are following Jesus.

Who are the leaders of groups
you belong to? What do they do?

WE BELIEVE

The Apostles led and cared for the Church.

Before Jesus died, he asked the Apostles to lead and care for all of his followers.
He chose the Apostle Peter to be the leader of all the Apostles.

 Matthew 16:18

Read Along

One day Jesus asked Peter what he believed. Peter said he believed that Jesus was the Son of God. Jesus then said to Peter, "And so I say to you, you are Peter, and upon this rock I will build my church." (Matthew 16:18)

The Holy Spirit helped Peter and all the Apostles to lead the Church. Their belief in Jesus stayed strong. They shared their love for Jesus with others.

The Apostles went to faraway lands to teach people about Jesus. Many of these people became members of the Church. The Apostles worked to help the Church grow.

Write one way you can share your love for Jesus with others this week.

_____

_____

The bishops lead and care for the Church.

Jesus chose the Apostles to lead the Church.
In later years, the Apostles chose other men
to lead the Church.
These men took the place of the Apostles.
They did the work the Apostles had done.
They worked together to lead the Church.
These leaders became known as bishops.

Bishops still lead and care
for the Church today.
They teach about Jesus and
the Church.
They pray with the people in
their care.

Bishops lead and care
for each diocese.
A diocese is made up of many
members of the Church.

Who is your bishop?
What is the name of your diocese?

109

The pope leads and cares for the whole Church.

The pope is the Bishop of Rome in Italy.
He takes the place of Saint Peter.
Just like Saint Peter, he leads and cares
for the whole Church.

The pope works together with
all the bishops.

- He prays for and takes care
  of the Church.

- He teaches what Jesus taught.

- He visits people all over the world.

- He helps people everywhere.

- He cares for those in need.

The Holy Spirit helps the pope
to care for the Church.

Imagine that you are
going to meet the pope.
What will you say to him?

As Catholics...

The pope lives in the Vatican
in Rome, Italy. The main church
building of the Vatican is called
Saint Peter's. It is named for Peter,
the first leader of the Church.

Find out the name of the pope.

The Church serves others.

Serving is another word for caring and helping others.

Read Along

Jesus showed his followers ways to serve others. He fed people who were hungry. He spent time with people who needed him. He took care of people who were sick. He shared God's love with everyone. Jesus said, "as I have done for you, you should also do." (John 13:15)

Members of the Church serve others. We show our love for God when we serve others.
How are the people in the pictures doing what Jesus did?

WE RESPOND

Put a ✔ beside each picture that shows how you and your family can love and serve others.

PROJECT

Show What *you* Know

Unscramble the words below. How have these people led and cared for the Church?

plostAse	hopsib	oppe

_____ _____ _____

- - - - - - - - - - - - - - - - - - - - - - - - - - - - - - - - - - - - - - -

_____ _____ _____

You are a member of the Church. Draw a picture of a way you can serve others.

DISCIPLE

Pray
Learn
Celebrate
Share
Choose
Live

Saint Stories Blessed Teresa of Calcutta was known as Mother Teresa. She cared for people in India who were sick and homeless. She and her helpers fed people. They gave them a place to stay. Mother Teresa's helpers are called the Missionaries of Charity. They care for people in cities all over the world.

More to Explore

What is the name of your bishop?
What is the name of the pope? Find out!

Take Home

Talk with your family about ways you can serve others. Make a plan!

↳ **DISCIPLE CHALLENGE**
Print your family name on the pledge card. Ask each family member to sign it.

The _____ Family pledges to serve others.

_____

_____

_____

CHAPTER TEST

Circle the correct answer.

1. Did Jesus choose Peter to be the leader of the Apostles?

Yes   **No**

2. Do we serve others by caring for and helping them?

Yes   **No**

3. Is the pope the leader of your town?

Yes   **No**

4. Do the bishops do the work the Apostles did?

Yes   **No**

5. Does the pope only care about some of the members of the Church?

Yes   **No**

 **TALK ABOUT IT** What are some ways the Church loves and serves others?

Come, Lord Jesus!
Be with us.

SEASONAL

CHAPTER 13

This chapter prepares us to celebrate
the season of Advent.

WE GATHER

Think about a time your family was waiting to celebrate a special day.

What did you do?

How did you feel?

WE BELIEVE

The Church has a special time of waiting. Each year we wait for the coming of the Son of God. This waiting time is called Advent.

The word *Advent* means "coming." Each year during Advent we prepare. We get ready for the coming of God's Son, Jesus. We get ready to celebrate his birth at Christmas.

There are four weeks in Advent. The Church celebrates these four weeks in different ways. One way is by lighting candles on an Advent wreath.

On the Advent wreath there is one candle for each week. The light from the candles reminds us that Jesus is the Light of the World.

We pray as we light the candles on the Advent wreath. We remember that Jesus is with us. We prepare to celebrate his birth at Christmas.

 Color the flames on each candle on the Advent wreath.

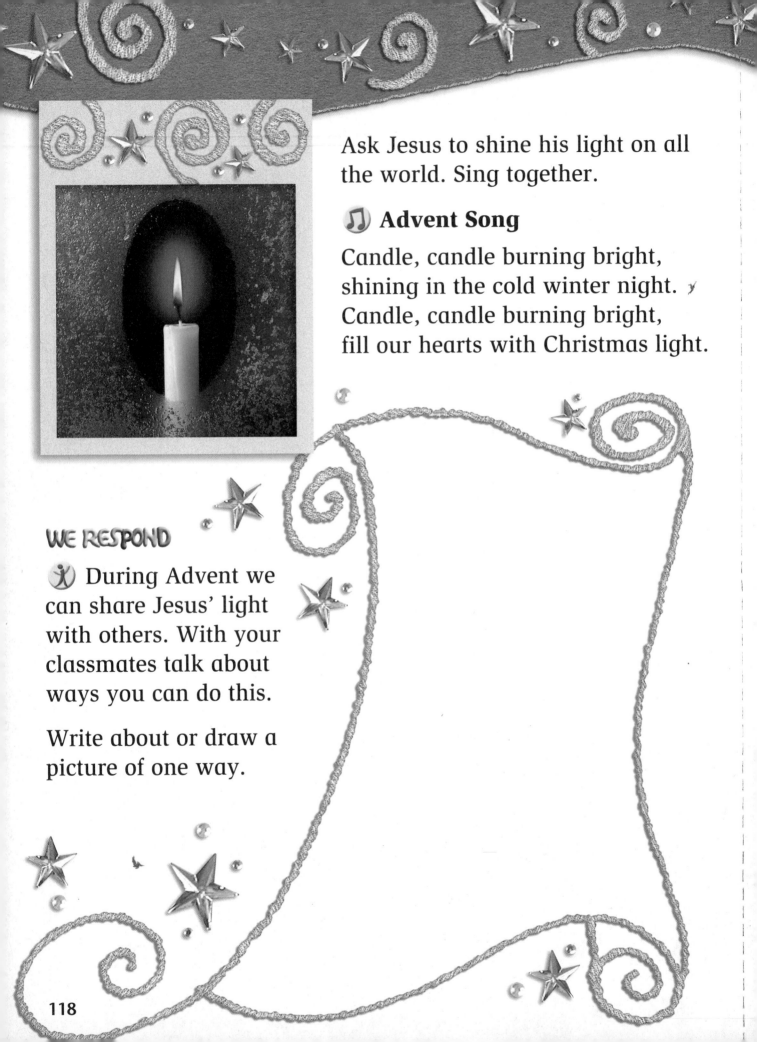

Ask Jesus to shine his light on all the world. Sing together.

🎵 **Advent Song**

Candle, candle burning bright,
shining in the cold winter night.
Candle, candle burning bright,
fill our hearts with Christmas light.

WE RESPOND

During Advent we can share Jesus' light with others. With your classmates talk about ways you can do this.

Write about or draw a picture of one way.

✝ We Respond in Prayer

Leader: Let us praise God and listen to his Word.

Reader: Jesus said, "I am the light of the world. Whoever follows me will not walk in darkness, but will have the light of life." (John 8:12)

The Gospel of the Lord.

All: Praise to you, Lord Jesus Christ.

Leader: Jesus, help us to make the world bright with your life.

All: Come, Lord Jesus!

♫ Jesus, Come to Us

Jesus, come to us,
lead us to your light.
Jesus, be with us,
for we need you.

PROJECT DISCIPLE

Picture This   Color by number.

Color 1  yellow

Color 2 pink

Color 3 purple

Color 4 green

Color 5 brown

↳ **DISCIPLE CHALLENGE** What does the picture show?

_____

- -

_____

Pray Today

Trace this prayer.

Pray it during Advent to show you are waiting for Jesus.

Come, Lord Jesus!

Take Home

How can your family share Jesus' light with others? Decide on one way and make it happen during the Advent season.

"For a child is born to us, a son is given us."

Isaiah 9:5

SEASONAL

CHAPTER 14

This chapter addresses the entire Christmas season.

At Christmas the Church celebrates the birth of Jesus.

WE GATHER

What do you think of when you think of Christmas?

WE BELIEVE

Christmas is a special time. During Christmas, we celebrate the birth of the Son of God. We celebrate God's greatest gift to us, his Son, Jesus.

Act out this Christmas play.

Narrator: Before Jesus was born, the ruler wanted to count all the people. Each man had to go back to the town his family came from to be counted. Joseph's family was from Bethlehem. So Joseph and Mary made the long journey to Bethlehem.

Joseph: Here we are, Mary! We're finally in Bethlehem! You must be very tired.

Mary: I'm all right, Joseph. It was a long journey. It will be so good to rest!

Joseph: Here is an inn. Maybe we can stay here.

Innkeeper: Not another traveler! What do you want?

Joseph: We need a place to stay.

Innkeeper: Sorry, there's no room left.

Joseph: Please, sir. My wife needs a place to rest. We're going to have a baby soon.

Innkeeper's Wife: We do have a place where the animals are kept. I put down fresh straw this morning. At least you can try to keep warm there.

Mary: Thank you for your kindness. May God bless you!

Narrator: So Joseph and Mary stayed there. Joseph made a place for the baby in the animals' feedbox. It is called a manger. He filled the manger with clean straw.

That night, Jesus was born. Mary and Joseph were filled with joy. They wrapped the baby in swaddling clothes and laid him in the manger.

Read Along

During Christmas, we sing with joy. Jesus has brought light and love into the world. He is with us now and forever.

Christmas is a time to honor the Holy Family. We remember the love of Mary and Joseph. We remember their love and care for Jesus.

WE RESPOND

Christmas is a time to share God's love with family and friends. Each thing you do for others can be a gift.

Color each gift box that shows a way you can share God's love. Then add your own way.

Each day during this time of year try to do these things.

Help keep my home clean.

Get along with everyone.

Pray for my family.

Share my things.

We Respond in Prayer

Leader: Let us give thanks for the Son of God brings light and love into the world. Rejoice in the Lord always.

All: Rejoice in the Lord always.

Reader: Let us listen to a reading from the Bible.

"The people who walked in darkness
   have seen a great light;
Upon those who dwelt in the land
   of gloom
   a light has shone.
You have brought them abundant joy
   and great rejoicing." (Isaiah 9:1–2)

The word of the Lord.

All: Thanks be to God.

🎵 **Joy to the World**

Joy to the world!
The Lord is come;
Let earth receive her King;
Let ev'ry heart prepare him room,
And heav'n and nature sing,
And heav'n and nature sing,
And heav'n, and heav'n and nature sing.

PROJECT DISCIPLE

Pray Learn Celebrate Share Choose Live

Fast Facts

During Christmas, many people use a nativity scene to remind them of Jesus' birth.

↳ **DISCIPLE CHALLENGE** Can you find the Holy Family in the nativity scene? Circle Jesus, Mary, and Joseph.

Question Corner

What are some ways your family celebrates Christmas?

❏ Exchange gifts to show our love

❏ Share special meals

❏ Decorate our home

❏ Pray

❏ Celebrate Jesus' birth

❏ Set up a nativity scene

❏ Go to Mass

Take Home

As a family, think of a special way you can share God's love with others during Christmas.

UNIT TEST

Fill in the circle beside the correct answer.

1. Jesus taught his followers how to _____.

   ○ pray   ○ read

2. Jesus told us that he was the _____.

   ○ pope   ○ Good Shepherd

3. The Church is all the people who believe in _____ and follow his teachings.

   ○ Peter   ○ Jesus

Circle the correct answer.

4. Is the Holy Spirit the Third Person of the Blessed Trinity?   **Yes**   **No**

5. Did Jesus choose John to be the leader of the Apostles?   **Yes**   **No**

6. Did Jesus' followers believe he was the Son of God?   **Yes**   **No**

continued on next page   **127**

Match each sentence to the correct picture.

7.

● Jesus invited people to be his followers.

8.

● Jesus taught his followers to pray.

9.

● The first members of the Church shared God's love with others.

10.

● The Holy Spirit came to Jesus' followers on Pentecost.

We Belong to the Church

UNIT 3

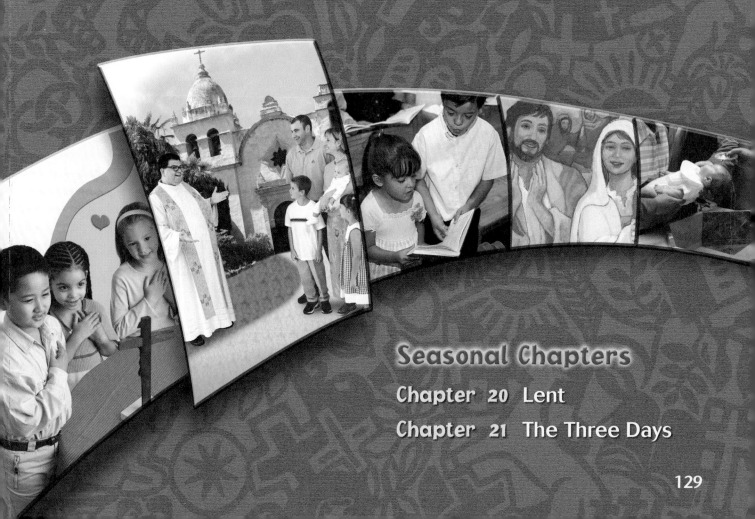

Seasonal Chapters

Pray
Learn
Celebrate
Share
Choose
Live

PROJECT DISCIPLE
DEAR FAMILY

In Unit 3 your child will grow as a disciple of Jesus by:

- appreciating the parish family and the ways the parish works and worships together
- celebrating God's love in the sacraments that Jesus gave us
- welcoming new members of the Church who receive Baptism
- choosing to act as "children of the light" by showing Christ to others
- understanding that God is always ready to forgive us and that he asks us to forgive others.

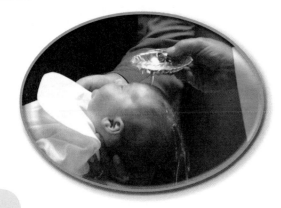

Question Corner

Which sacraments have your family members received?

Baptism _____

Confirmation _____

Penance _____

Eucharist _____

Matrimony _____

Holy Orders _____

Anointing of the Sick _____

Give thanks to Jesus for all the sacraments.

130

Reality Check

The Christian family "is a community of faith, hope, and charity; it assumes singular importance in the Church."

(*Catechism of the Catholic Church*, 2204)

More to Explore

Chapter 15 focuses on the parish. Name your parish. What other parishes do you know about? You might check your diocesan Web site. Talk about other parishes you have belonged to and the parishes in the neighborhoods around yours. How does your parish work with other parishes? Help your child to feel the connections we all have as Catholics.

Make it Happen

Talk about God's love and forgiveness. Remind your child how important forgiveness is in our relationship with God and with others. Is there anyone you need to say "I am sorry" to? Is there anyone you need to say "I forgive you" to? Make it happen!

Take Home

Each chapter in your child's *We Believe* Grade 1 text offers a "Take Home" activity that invites your family to support your child's journey to more fully become a disciple of Christ.

Be ready for this unit's Take Home:

Chapter 15: Helping people who are hungry

Chapter 16: Singing at Mass

Chapter 17: Finding holy water in your parish church

Chapter 18: Praying to Jesus, the Light of the World

Chapter 19: Forgiving others in the family

We Belong to a Parish

WE GATHER

✝ **Leader:** Jesus' followers said to him,
"Lord, teach us to pray." (Luke 11:1)
Let us join together and pray
the prayer Jesus taught.

All: Our Father, who art in heaven,
hallowed be thy name;
thy kingdom come;
thy will be done on earth
 as it is in heaven.
Give us this day our daily bread;
and forgive us our trespasses
as we forgive those who
 trespass against us;
and lead us not into temptation,
but deliver us from evil.
Amen.

What are some things
families do together?

WE BELIEVE

Our parish is like a family.

We belong to the Catholic Church.
We are Catholics. We belong to a parish.

A **parish** is a group of Catholics who join together to share God's love. They pray, celebrate, and work together.

We do many things with our parish.

- We praise and thank God.
- We share God's love with others.
- We learn how to be followers of Jesus.
- We work together to help people.

What things do you like to do with your parish?

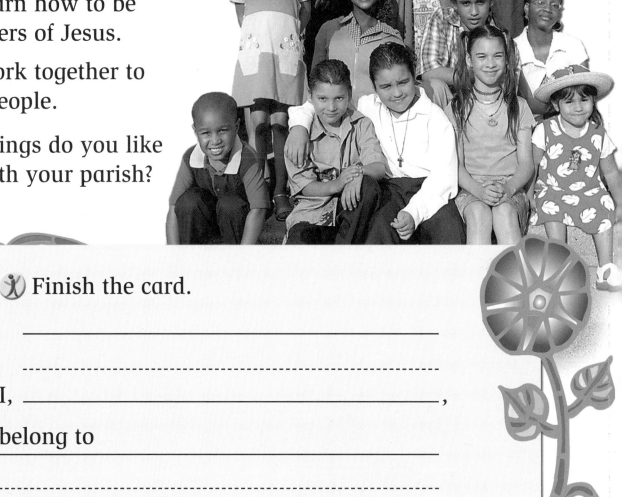

Finish the card.

_____

- -

I, _____,

belong to

_____

- -

_____ Parish.

We gather together to worship.

Our parish joins together to celebrate God's love. We **worship** God. We give him thanks and praise.

Every week we gather to worship God in our parish church. Our parish church is a holy place. God is with us there in a special way.

 **Open Our Hearts**

God, we come to worship you:

Chorus
Open our hearts to listen to you.
Open our hearts to listen to you.

God, your love is always true:
(Chorus)

133

We work together as a parish.

The leader of a parish is called the **pastor**. The pastor is a priest. The pastor leads us in worship. He teaches us about Jesus. He helps us to care for one another.

Sometimes the parish has a deacon. He helps the pastor. Other leaders in the parish work with the pastor, too. Together they help the parish family. Some help us to worship God. Some teach us about God. Some work with us to care for those who are sick or in need.

Key Word

pastor the priest who is the leader of the parish

Talk about ways you can thank your pastor and the people who help him.

As Catholics...

Catechists teach the Catholic faith to the children, youth, and adults of the parish. They are very important people in the parish. They teach about Jesus and the Church. They help us to be friends and followers of Jesus.

Who teaches you about the Catholic faith?

Our parish helps many people.

We spend time with our parish family. We help people of our parish who are in need.

Our parish helps other people, too. We gather food and clothes for those who are poor. We send money to those who are in need.

Our parish cares for those who are sick. People visit them. We pray for them.

WE RESPOND

Circle one way you will help your parish this week.

- Join in singing and praying.
- Pray for my parish.
- Be kind and friendly.

Together say a prayer for all those who are in need.

PROJECT

Show What *you* Know

Draw a line to match the Key Word puzzle pieces.

pastor • • to give God thanks and praise

parish • • the priest who is the leader of the parish

worship • • a group of Catholics who join together to share God's love

DISCIPLE

Pray
Learn
Celebrate
Share
Choose
Live

Make *it* Happen

Think about the people in your parish. Answer each question.

Who helps you worship God?

Who teaches you about God?

Who cares for those who need help?

↳ **DISCIPLE CHALLENGE** Thank these people for the special work they do.

Reality Check

How is your parish like a family?

❏ We belong together.

❏ We help each other.

❏ We share God's love.

❏ We pray together.

Take Home

Some people do not have homes or jobs. These people need food. Many parish families join together to help people who are hungry. Some cook and serve meals to people who come to eat at a soup kitchen. Some collect food for the hungry. How can your family help people who are hungry?

Circle the correct answer.

1. Do the people in a parish pray, celebrate, and work together?

Yes   **No**

2. Is a parish church a holy place?

Yes   **No**

3. Is the president the priest who leads the parish?

Yes   **No**

4. Do the people in a parish help many people?

Yes   **No**

5. Do we forget about God when we worship him?

Yes   **No**

 **TALK ABOUT IT** What do the people in your parish do together?

We Celebrate the Sacraments

16

WE GATHER

✝ **Leader:** There are many signs of God's love for us. We see God's love in his gifts of creation and in one another. Jesus is the greatest sign of God's love. He shares God's life and love with us. Let us celebrate God's love for us.

🎵 **We Celebrate With Joy**

Chorus

We celebrate with joy and gladness
We celebrate God's love for us.
We celebrate with joy and gladness
God with us today. (Clap 2 times.)
God with us today. (Clap 2 times.)

God before us. God behind us.
God in everything we do.
God before us. God behind us.
God in all we do. (Chorus)

 What special times does your family celebrate?

WE BELIEVE

Jesus celebrated God's love.

Jesus celebrated special times with his family and friends. He celebrated Jewish feasts. He gathered with others to worship God. Together they celebrated God's love. Together they prayed songs of praise.

Here is one of these songs of praise.

Psalm 100:1–2

"Shout joyfully to the LORD,
    all you lands;
  worship the LORD with cries
    of gladness;
  come before him with joyful song."

Sometimes we pray these words when we worship God as a parish.

Pray together the song of praise above. Make up actions for the prayer.

140

We celebrate God's love.

We gather with our parish family to worship together. We thank God for sending his Son. We remember the things that Jesus said and did. We ask the Holy Spirit to help us.

When we worship, we pray with special songs, words, and actions. We stand and pray. We pray Alleluia and Amen.

When we worship God together, we ask God to be with us. We listen to God's Word.

Draw yourself worshiping God with your parish.

Jesus gave us the sacraments.

Jesus, the Son of God, wants each of us to share in God's life. So he gave us seven special signs of God's life and love. The seven special signs Jesus gave us are called sacraments. A **sacrament** is a special sign given to us by Jesus.

We gather with our parish family to celebrate the sacraments. Jesus is with us each time we celebrate.

👥 Talk about ways you can thank Jesus for giving us the sacraments.

① Baptism

Eucharist ③

Confirmation ④

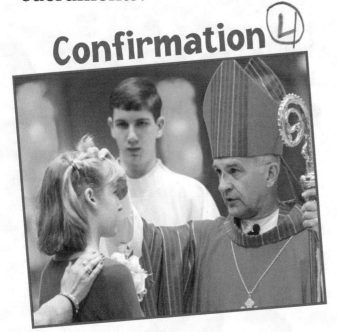

As Catholics...

We use the gifts of God's creation during the celebration of the sacraments. For example, water and oils are used to bless us. Light from candles reminds us that Jesus is with us. Bread made from wheat and wine made from grapes are used, too.

With your family, thank God for all he has given us.

The Church celebrates Seven Sacraments.

The Church celebrates Seven Sacraments. Jesus shares God's life with us in each of the sacraments.

⑦ **Anointing of the Sick**

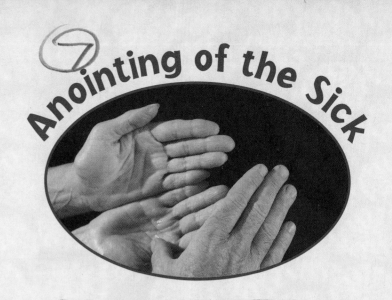

② **Penance and Reconciliation**

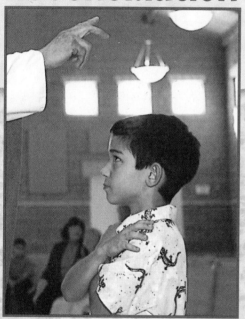

⑥ **Holy Orders**

WE RESPOND

Talk about what sacrament is being celebrated in each picture on these pages.

✺ Circle any sacrament you have received.

⑤ **Matrimony**

143

PROJECT

Show What *you* Know

Go back in your chapter and draw a [   ] around the Key Word sacrament.

Picture This

Match the picture of the sacrament to its name.

● **Penance and Reconciliation**

● **Matrimony**

● **Baptism**

Pray
Learn
Celebrate
Share
Choose
Live

Question Corner

Show this chart to friends and family members. Ask each person, "Which is your favorite way to celebrate God's love?" Each time someone names one of the actions, put a mark in the space below it.

sing	pray	listen	gather

↳ DISCIPLE CHALLENGE Count up the marks in each box. Which action is the most popular?

Fast Facts

You can celebrate God's love at Mass every week.

Take Home

Some people use their talent to write songs of praise and thanks to God. We sing some of these songs when our parish family gathers to worship God. We sing these songs when we celebrate the sacraments. The next time you are at Mass, listen for these songs of praise and thanks to God. Join in the singing!

Circle the correct answer.

1. Jesus shares God's life with us in _____ of the sacraments.

each   some

2. _____ gave us the sacraments.

Peter   Jesus

3. The Church celebrates _____ Sacraments.

Seven   Ten

4. _____ is a special word we use when we worship God.

Hello   Alleluia

5. Jesus _____ gather with others to worship God.

did   did not

 What are some of the special words and actions we use to worship God?

The Church Welcomes New Members

17

WE GATHER

✝ **Leader:** God the Father,
   All: We praise you.

Leader: Jesus, Son of God,
   All: Show us how to live.

Leader: God the Holy Spirit,
   All: Help us each day.

☀ What do families do to welcome new babies?

WE BELIEVE

The Church welcomes new members at Baptism.

Father Marcos and the whole parish are welcoming the Stanik family. They are bringing Baby Leo to celebrate the Sacrament of Baptism.

Baptism is the sacrament in which we become children of God and members of the Church. Baptism is the first sacrament we receive.

When we were baptized, we became children of God. We became members of the Church, too. We celebrated Baptism with our parish family. They welcomed us into the Catholic Church.

 Talk about why you think Baptism is so important.

As Catholics...

We receive the Sacrament of Baptism once. Some people are baptized when they are babies. Others are baptized when they are older. Older children, teenagers, or adults are usually baptized at a celebration on the night before Easter Sunday.

How old were you when you were baptized?

At Baptism we receive God's life.

Water is an important sign of Baptism. During the sacrament we are placed in water, or water is poured on us.

This happens in a special place in our parish church. This place is called the baptismal pool or font.

Water is a sign of the life God gives us. At Baptism God gives us a share in his life. We call God's life in us **grace**.

Grace helps us to grow as God's children. It helps us to grow as followers of Jesus.

Key Words

Baptism the sacrament in which we become children of God and members of the Church.

grace God's life in us

🧍 Water reminds us of our Baptism. Color the water at the bottom of these pages. Thank God for his gift of grace.

We say and do special things to celebrate Baptism.

The Church celebrates Baptism with special words and actions.

Read Along

Leo's Baptism

Father Marcos traced the sign of the cross on Leo's forehead. Leo's parents and godparents did, too. This showed that Leo would soon be a follower of Jesus.

Father poured water on Leo's head three times. He said the words of Baptism:

> Leo, I baptize you in the name
>   of the Father,
> and of the Son,
> and of the Holy Spirit.

Each of us was baptized with water and these words, too.

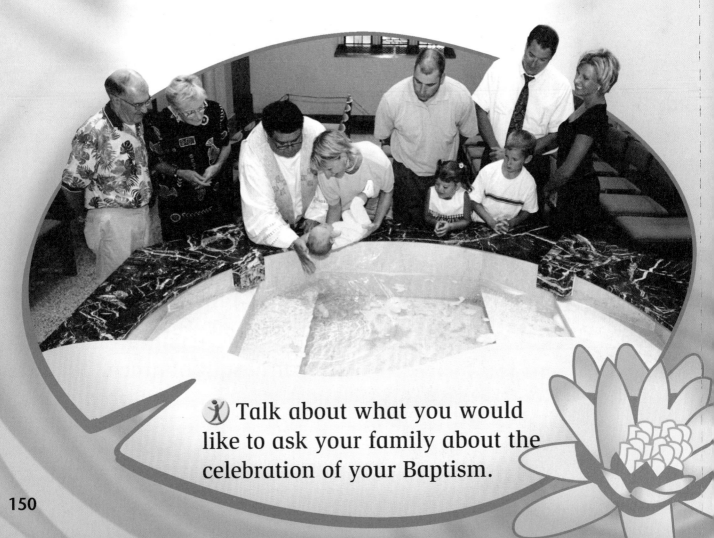

Talk about what you would like to ask your family about the celebration of your Baptism.

In Baptism we are joined to Jesus and one another.

Read Along

A white garment was put on Leo. Father prayed that Leo would always live as a follower of Jesus.

A candle was given to Leo's family. Father prayed that Leo would always walk in the light of Christ.

Everyone prayed the Lord's Prayer.

These same words and actions were part of the celebration of our Baptism.

As baptized members of the Church, we help one another to follow Jesus. We share in God's life together. We share our beliefs.

WE RESPOND

What will you do to live as a follower of Jesus?

 Decorate this candle.

I will walk in the light of Christ.

151

PROJECT

Show What you Know

Use the **Key Words** to complete the puzzle.

Baptism
grace

1 Across: God's life in us

2 Down: The sacrament in which we become children of God and members of the Church

```
        2 [ ]
        [ ]
1 [ ][ ][ ][ ]
        [ ]
        [ ]
        [ ]
        [ ]
        [ ]
```

Celebrate!

Decorate a Baptism banner to welcome a new member of the Church. Use pictures and words.

↳ **DISCIPLE CHALLENGE** Learn more about your own Baptism. Ask your parents and godparents.

DISCIPLE

Pray
Learn
Celebrate
Share
Choose
Live

Picture This

Number the pictures of Leo's Baptism to put them in order. Two are done for you.

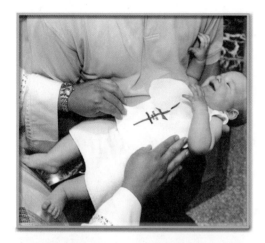

3

_____

1

_____

Take Home

Holy water is water that has been blessed by a priest. The priest traces a cross over the water with his hand. He says a special prayer. Holy water is kept in a special container in church. With your family, find the holy water in your parish church.

CHAPTER TEST

Circle the correct answer.

1. Is Baptism the third sacrament we receive?

Yes   No

2. Is water an important sign of Baptism?

Yes   No

3. Do we become members of the Church in Baptism?

Yes   No

4. Is grace God's life in us?

Yes   No

5. Does the Church celebrate Baptism with special words and actions?

Yes   No

 **TALK ABOUT IT** Why are we given a white garment and a candle at Baptism?

We Are Followers of Jesus

WE GATHER

✝ **Leader:** Let us listen to the Word of God.

 John 8:12

Read Along

One day Jesus was talking to a crowd. He said to them, "I am the light of the world. Whoever follows me will not walk in darkness, but will have the light of life."

🎵 **Walk in the Light**

Jesus is the Light for all:
Walk, walk in the light!
We follow him as we hear
    his call.
Walk, walk in the light!

Walk, walk in the light!
(Sing 3 times.)

Walk in the light
    of the Lord!

☀ How does
    light help us?

155

Jesus is the Light of the World.

 John 8:12

Read Along

One day Jesus was talking to a crowd. He said to them, "I am the light of the world. Whoever follows me will not walk in darkness, but will have the light of life." (John 8:12)

We believe that Jesus is the Light of the World. He helps us to see what God's love is like. He shares God's life with us.

Jesus wants us to follow him. If we follow him, we will have life with God.

🏃 Draw a picture to show that Jesus is the Light of the World.

We receive the light of Christ.

When we are baptized, we receive the light of Christ. We are told to "walk always as children of the light."

As children of the light we:

- believe in Jesus
- act as Jesus wants us to
- love one another.

We show others the light of Christ when we:

- help our family and friends
- share what we have with others
- care about the ways others feel.

Talk about ways the people in the photos are sharing the light of Christ.

Jesus asks us to share his peace.

Jesus wanted his followers to be at peace. He wanted them to live in God's love. He wanted them to show love for one another.

 Matthew 5:1, 9

Read Along

One day Jesus went up a mountain. There he spoke to many people. He told them:
"Blessed are the peacemakers,
for they will be called children of God." (Matthew 5:9)

Jesus wants us to work for peace. A person who works for peace is a **peacemaker**.

We are peacemakers when we say and do kind things for others. We work for peace when we try to get along with all people.

Act out one way you can share peace with one another.

Key Word

peacemaker a person who works for peace

As Catholics...

Guiseppe Sarto was born in Italy. When he was growing up, he tried to be kind to all people.

He studied and became a priest. Years later he was chosen to be the pope. He was called Pope Pius X. Pope Pius X heard that many countries were going to have a war. He tried to be a peacemaker. He met with the leaders of these countries. He tried to stop them from fighting. Pope Pius X wanted all countries to get along.

Who are other people in our world who work for peace?

We can make choices as children of God.

God loves us very much. We are different from the rest of his creation. We are special. We can make choices.

Sometimes we make choices without even thinking about them. But God wants us to think about the things we say and do.

God asks us to choose to love him and others. He wants us to choose to do what Jesus taught us.

WE RESPOND

 You want to use your sister's book. Circle the loving choice.

- You choose to ask your sister.

- You choose to just take the book.

Talk about what you think. Is it always easy to make loving choices?

Show What *you* Know

Who is a person who works for peace?

_____

- -

_____

Picture This

On the candle write three ways that you can share the light of Christ.

DISCIPLE

Pray
Learn
Celebrate
Share
Choose
Live

What Would *you* do?

William and Rebecca are arguing in the playground. What could you do as a peacemaker? Add yourself to the picture.

More *to* Explore

Work with a friend. Who is a peacemaker in the world today? Write the person's name or draw a picture of the person in the heart.

Take Home

People all over the world gather to share Jesus' light by praying together. Sometimes people hold candles or other kinds of lights as they pray. Try this with your family. Gather together to pray. Use candles or other lights. As you pray, remember that Jesus is the Light of the World.

CHAPTER TEST

Circle the correct answer.

1. Is Jesus the Light of the World?

Yes   **No**

2. Do we show others the light of Christ when we tell lies?

Yes   **No**

3. Are we peacemakers when we fight?

Yes   **No**

4. Can we make choices to love God and others?

Yes   **No**

5. Do we receive the light of Christ at Baptism?

Yes   **No**

 Talk about ways we can work for peace at home, in school, and in our neighborhoods.

We Celebrate God's Forgiveness

WE GATHER

✝ **Leader:** Holy Spirit, be with us now. Help us to think about ways we have or have not followed Jesus this week.

All: Holy Spirit, help us.

Leader: As I read these questions, pray to God quietly.

- Do I take time to pray?
- Am I kind to others?
- Do I listen to those who take care of me?
- Do I help people who need help?
- Do I tell the truth?

All: God, we are sorry for the times we have not loved you or others. Thank you for always loving us. We want to keep growing in your love.

☀ How do you show that you forgive others?

WE BELIEVE

Jesus told us about God's forgiveness.

Jesus told stories about God's love and forgiveness.

Here is one story.

Luke 15:11–23

Read Along

A loving father had two sons. One day, the younger son asked his father for money. The son took the money and left home. He spent the money having fun.

Soon all the money was gone. The young man had nowhere to live and nothing to eat. He knew that what he had done had hurt his father. He wanted to go home and tell his father how sorry he was.

When the young man was near his home, his father ran out to meet him. He gave him a big hug. He was so glad to see his son again. The son told his father he was sorry. The father said, "Let us celebrate with a feast." (Luke 15:23)

Jesus told this story to teach us that God always loves us. God is like the forgiving father in this story.

Put a ♥ by the picture that shows the father forgiving his son.

God is always ready to forgive us.

Jesus followed God's laws. He wants us to follow God's laws, too.

Sometimes we choose not to follow God's laws. We do things that do not show love for God and others.

Jesus taught us to ask God to forgive us. God always forgives us if we are sorry.

🎵 Children of God

Chorus
> Children of God in one family,
> loved by God in one family.
> And no matter what we do
> God loves me and
> God loves you.

Jesus teaches us to love.
Sometimes we get it wrong.
But God forgives us ev'ry time
  for we belong to the (Chorus).

We celebrate God's forgiveness.

Jesus gave us a way to ask God for forgiveness. It is the Sacrament of **Penance and Reconciliation**. We can call this sacrament the Sacrament of Penance.

Read Along

In this sacrament we receive and celebrate God's forgiveness. We do these things.

- We think about what we have said and done. We are sorry for the times we have not loved God and others.

- We meet with the priest.

- We listen to a story from the Bible about God's forgiveness.

- We talk to the priest about what we have done. We tell God we are sorry.

- The priest shares God's forgiveness with us.

 Talk about ways we can tell God we are sorry. Tell your family about God's love and forgiveness.

As Catholics...

We usually celebrate the Sacrament of Penance in our parish church. There is a special place in church where we meet with the priest. Here we can talk with the priest face-to-face, or we can talk from behind a screen.

Where is the Sacrament of Penance celebrated in your parish church?

Penance and Reconciliation the sacrament in which we receive and celebrate God's forgiveness

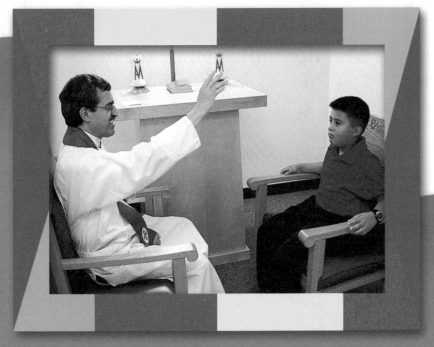

166

Jesus asks us to forgive others.

When we celebrate the Sacrament of Penance, we receive God's forgiveness and peace. Jesus told his followers that it is important to forgive others. He wants us to share God's peace.

WE RESPOND

Ask the Holy Spirit to help you to be loving and forgiving.

Read Along

Your little brother left your favorite book outside. It started raining. All the pages got wet. Then your brother said, "I am sorry. Please forgive me."

 What would you say to be forgiving? Circle the words.

- "I am going to break one of your toys."

- "I liked that book, but I forgive you."

- "Go away. I do not want to talk to you."

PROJECT

Show What you Know

Fill in the missing letters to read an important message.

I can receive and celebrate God's forgiveness in the Sacrament of

__ e __ a __ c __ a __ __ __
__ e __ o __ __ i __ ia __ io __.

I am Sorry

Reality Check

Check your favorite way to tell someone you are sorry.

❑ Please forgive me.

❑ I am sorry.

❑ I apologize for what I did.

↳ **DISCIPLE CHALLENGE** Remember to tell God and others when you are sorry.

DISCIPLE

Pray
Learn
Celebrate
Share
Choose
Live

Make *it* Happen

Write a forgiveness picture story in the space below. Be sure to include a beginning, a middle, and an end to your story.

beginning	middle	end

Take Home

Invite your family to make a chart at home that tallies the number of times family members forgive each other. When someone forgives, he or she puts a checkmark on the chart.

CHAPTER TEST

Circle the correct answer.

1. Jesus told stories about God's love and _____.

forgetting   forgiveness

2. In one of Jesus' stories God is like the _____.

son   forgiving father

3. God is _____ ready to forgive us.

always   sometimes

4. In the Sacrament of Penance, we _____ and celebrate God's forgiveness.

receive   return

5. It is _____ to forgive others.

not important   important

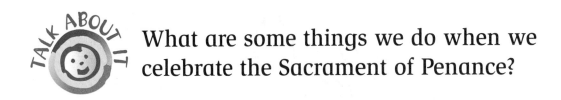 What are some things we do when we celebrate the Sacrament of Penance?

A good samaritan

"Try to learn what is pleasing to the Lord."

Ephesians 5:10

SEASONAL

CHAPTER 20

This chapter offers preparation for the season of Lent.

WE GATHER

When do you remember what your family has done for you? When do you remember what God has done for you?

WE BELIEVE

Lent is a special time in the Church. We remember all that Jesus has done for us. We get ready for the Church's great celebration of Jesus' Death and Resurrection.

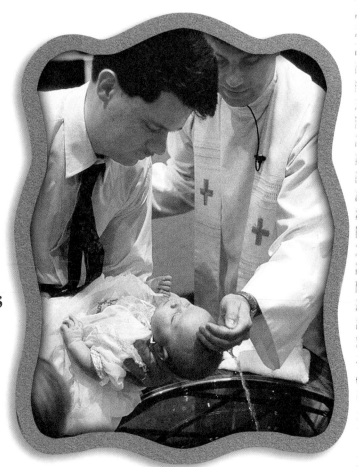

Lent is a time to remember our Baptism. In Baptism we first received grace, the gift of God's life. During Lent we praise Jesus for sharing his life with us.

We were baptized in the name of the Father, and of the Son, and of the Holy Spirit. Praying the Sign of the Cross reminds us of our Baptism.

Talk about the special things that happened at your Baptism.

Close your eyes. Thank Jesus for sharing his life with you. Now pray together the Sign of the Cross.

During Lent we try to grow closer to Jesus. We pray and follow his example. We thank God for his great love. We celebrate God's forgiveness. We help people who are sick, hungry, and lonely.

Followers of Jesus Christ should always do these things. However, they have special meaning when we do them during Lent.

Look at the pictures on this page. Act out what the people in the pictures are doing and saying.

WE RESPOND

Each time you do something to grow closer to Jesus during Lent, color one of the spaces in this cross.

WE RESPOND

174

✝ We Respond in Prayer

Leader: The Lord calls us to days of quiet time, prayer, and kind acts. Blessed be the name of the Lord.

All: Now and for ever.

Leader: During this time of Lent we trust in God's love and forgiveness.

All: Happy are those who trust in the Lord.

Leader: Together we pray as Jesus taught us.

All: Our Father, who art in heaven,
hallowed be thy name;
thy kingdom come;
thy will be done on earth as it is
in heaven.
Give us this day our daily bread;
and forgive us our trespasses
as we forgive those who trespass
against us;
and lead us not into temptation,
but deliver us from evil.
Amen.

Celebrate!

Draw yourself doing something that brings you closer to Jesus during Lent.

Pray Today

Finish this prayer.

Jesus, thank you for sharing your

_____

- -

_____.

Thank you for giving me

_____

- -

_____.

Amen.

Take Home

Talk about ways your family can grow closer to Jesus during Lent.

Plan to make one of these ways happen.

Lord, through your cross you brought joy to the world.

SEASONAL

CHAPTER 21

This chapter includes the three days from Holy Thursday evening until Easter Sunday.

The Church celebrates that Jesus died and rose to new life.

WE GATHER

Think about the crosses that you see. How are they different?

WE BELIEVE

Lent is a time that gets us ready for the Church's greatest celebration. Lent gets us ready for the great Three Days. These Three Days celebrate Jesus' dying and rising to new life.

During the Three Days, we gather with our parish. We celebrate at night and during the day.

We do the things Jesus asked us to do. We remember that Jesus gave himself to us at the Last Supper. We remember the ways Jesus loved and served others.

We listen to readings from the Bible. We pray before the cross. The cross reminds us of Jesus' dying and rising to new life.

Draw a picture here to show one way you will celebrate the Three Days with your parish.

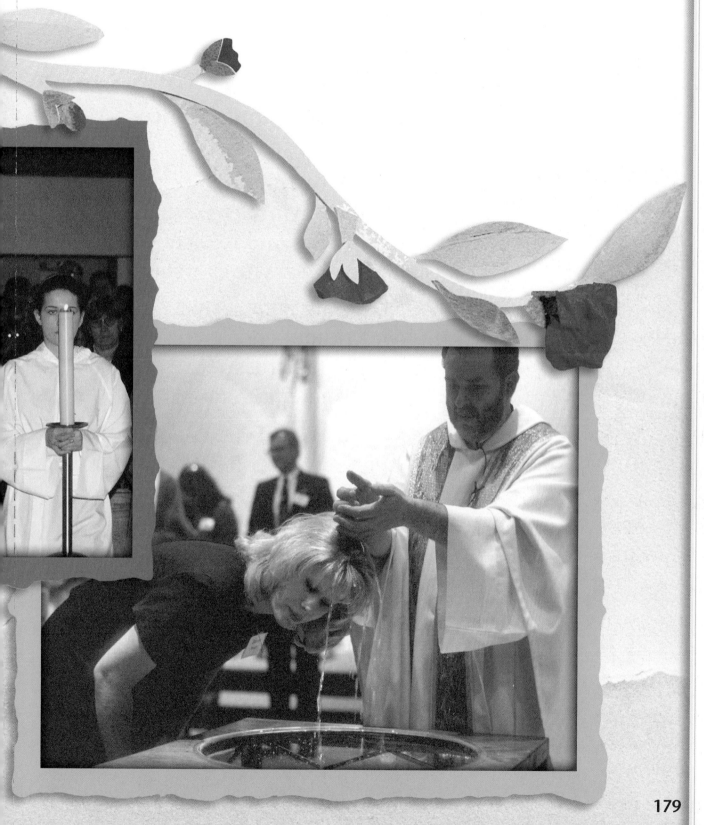

We sing with joy to celebrate that Jesus rose from the dead. We remember our Baptism in a special way. We welcome new members into the Church. We celebrate with songs of joy and praise.

WE RESPOND

🎵 **Awake! Arise, and Rejoice**

Chorus

Awake! Arise, and rejoice!
This is the day of the Lord!
Awake! Arise, and rejoice!
Open the gates with our song!

We sing now with Jesus,
of love without end;
we sing of the cross
and of rising again. (Chorus)

HOLY! HOLY!

✝ We Respond in Prayer

Leader: Lord, through your cross
you brought joy to the world.

All: Lord, through your cross
you brought joy to the world.

Leader: Holy is God!

All: Holy is God!

Leader: Holy and strong!

All: Holy and strong!

🎵 **Shout from the Mountains**

And we sing:
Holy, holy,
holy is God!
Holy, holy,
holy and strong!

HOLY!

PROJECT DISCIPLE

Celebrate!

Match the pictures to the ways that we can celebrate the Three Days.

● Pray before the cross.

● Remember that Jesus gave himself to us.

● Remember our Baptism.

Take Home

Mark the Three Days on your family calendar. Remember to celebrate with your parish on these days.

Draw a line to match the sentence parts.

1. Jesus is ● ● we use special words and actions.

2. Every week our parish gathers ● ● are called sacraments.

3. When we worship ● ● we become members of the Church.

4. The seven special signs Jesus gave us ● ● to worship God.

5. When we are baptized ● ● the Light of the World.

continued on next page **183**

Read the sentences below.

Use a  blue to circle the ones about **Baptism**.

Use a purple to circle the ones about **Penance**.

6. We are welcomed to the Church.

7. We tell God we are sorry.

8. We are invited to walk in the light of Christ.

9. Water is a sign of the life God gives us.

10. The priest shares God's forgiveness with us.

We Celebrate and Live Our Faith

UNIT 4

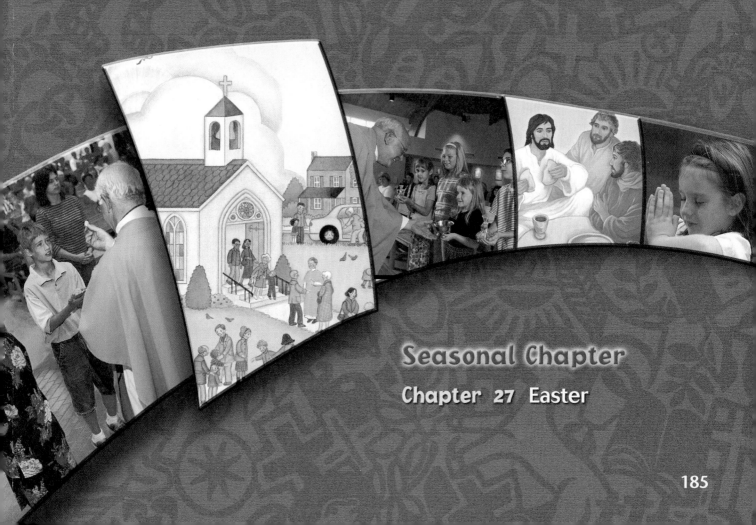

Seasonal Chapter

DEAR FAMILY

In Unit 4 your child will grow as a disciple of Jesus by:

- appreciating that at Mass we celebrate what Jesus did at the Last Supper
- gathering with the parish family for the celebration of the Mass
- sharing God's love by loving and serving our family and others
- honoring Mary and all the saints by asking them to pray for us and by following their example
- caring for all of God's creation, and respecting all people as Jesus taught us to do.

Saint Stories

Introduce your child to Saint Jerome who is the Patron of Scripture Scholars. As a young student, he learned Latin and Greek and later translated the Bible into Latin. He said, "Now we must translate the words of Scripture into deeds, and instead of speaking holy words, we must do them." What words of Scripture can you do today? Pray to Saint Jerome before the Liturgy of the Word at Mass this Sunday.

Celebrate!

In Chapter 22, your child is reminded of the Third Commandment, "Remember to keep holy the Lord's Day." Participating in the Sunday celebration of the Mass is the first way we keep the Lord's Day holy. We can also spend time together as a family and do something for those in need. Plan to make this Sunday holy by doing all of these!

Reality Check

"Parents should initiate their children at an early age into the mysteries of the faith of which they are the 'first heralds' for their children."

(*Catechism of the Catholic Church*, 2225)

Picture This

Chapter 23 has photos of what happens at Mass. Look at the pictures together, and ask your child about what is happening in each one. How are the photos like what happens at your parish? How are they different?

Show That You Care

At the end of Mass, we often hear these words: "Go in peace." What are some ways in which your family shows love for the Lord and serves him? Choose one special way you will love and serve the Lord this week.

Take Home

Each chapter in your child's *We Believe* Grade 1 text offers a "Take Home" activity that invites your family to support your child's journey to more fully become a disciple of Christ.

Be ready for this unit's Take Home:

Chapter 22: Listing people who help us worship at Mass

Chapter 23: Praying for parishioners who are sick

Chapter 24: Sharing God's love as a family

Chapter 25: Making a family tree

Chapter 26: Caring for God's creation

Jesus Gives Us the Eucharist

WE GATHER

✝ **Leader:** Let us join hands and form a circle of friends.

Reader 1: O God, we gather now to pray.

All: We praise you together.

Reader 2: We listen to your Word.

All: We praise you together.

Reader 3: We lift up our hearts.

All: We praise you together.

Reader 4: We share your love with everyone.

All: We praise you together.

☀ What are some things people do to celebrate holidays?

WE BELIEVE

Jesus shared a special meal with his followers.

On the night before he died, Jesus was with his followers in Jerusalem. They were celebrating a Jewish holiday with a special meal. Here is what Jesus said and did.

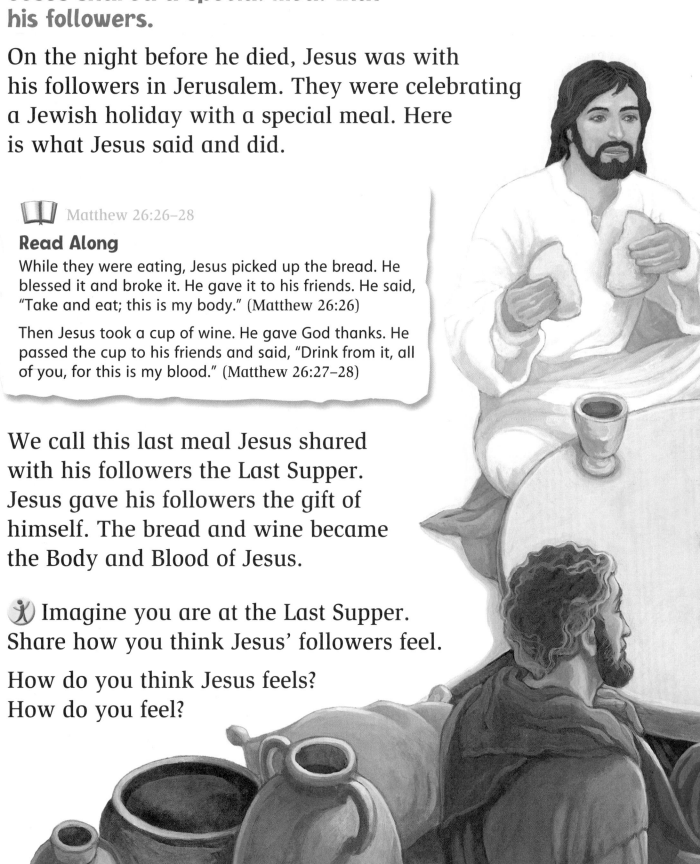

Matthew 26:26–28

Read Along

While they were eating, Jesus picked up the bread. He blessed it and broke it. He gave it to his friends. He said, "Take and eat; this is my body." (Matthew 26:26)

Then Jesus took a cup of wine. He gave God thanks. He passed the cup to his friends and said, "Drink from it, all of you, for this is my blood." (Matthew 26:27–28)

We call this last meal Jesus shared with his followers the Last Supper. Jesus gave his followers the gift of himself. The bread and wine became the Body and Blood of Jesus.

Imagine you are at the Last Supper. Share how you think Jesus' followers feel.

How do you think Jesus feels?
How do you feel?

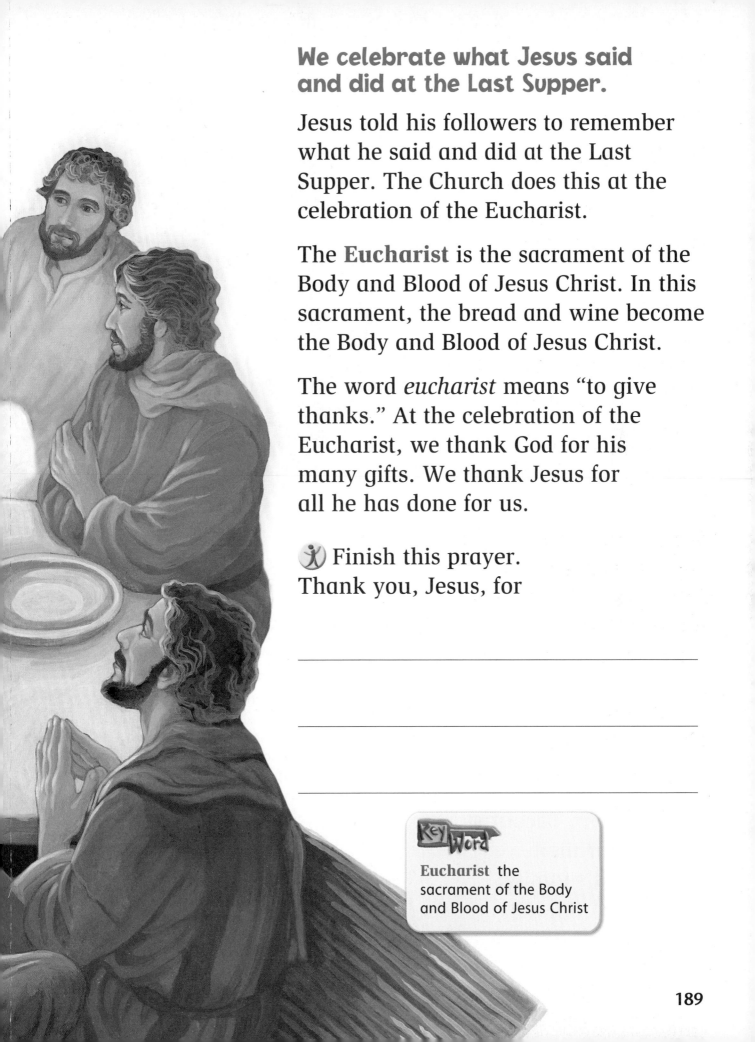

We celebrate what Jesus said and did at the Last Supper.

Jesus told his followers to remember what he said and did at the Last Supper. The Church does this at the celebration of the Eucharist.

The **Eucharist** is the sacrament of the Body and Blood of Jesus Christ. In this sacrament, the bread and wine become the Body and Blood of Jesus Christ.

The word *eucharist* means "to give thanks." At the celebration of the Eucharist, we thank God for his many gifts. We thank Jesus for all he has done for us.

Finish this prayer.
Thank you, Jesus, for

_____

_____

_____

Key Word

Eucharist the sacrament of the Body and Blood of Jesus Christ

We celebrate the Sacrament of the Eucharist.

The **Mass** is another name for the celebration of the Eucharist. The Mass is the Church's greatest celebration.

At Mass we worship God together. We praise the Father for his love. We celebrate the life of his Son, Jesus. We ask the Holy Spirit to help us celebrate.

Jesus is with us in a special way at Mass. He is with us

- when we gather together

- when we listen to God's Word

- when we remember what Jesus said and did at the Last Supper

- when we share his Body and Blood.

🎵 We Come to Share God's Special Gift

We come to share God's special gift:
Jesus here in Eucharist
for you, for me,
for all God's family;
for me, for you
God's love is always true!

As Catholics...

The Third Commandment is: Remember to keep holy the Lord's Day. For the Church, Sunday is the Lord's Day. This is because Jesus rose to new life on a Sunday.

The Lord's Day begins on Saturday evening and ends on Sunday evening. During this time we gather with our parish to celebrate Mass. This celebration is the greatest way we can keep the Lord's Day holy.

What are some other ways you can keep Sunday holy?

We join with our parish for the celebration of Mass.

Every Sunday we gather as a parish to celebrate Mass. A priest leads us in this celebration. We take part in the celebration of the Mass. We sing and pray. We listen to God's Word.

We offer our prayers to God. The priest does what Jesus did at the Last Supper. Then we are sent out to share God's love with others.

WE RESPOND

What can you do to take part in the celebration of Mass?

Mass another name for the celebration of the Eucharist

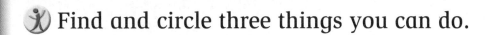 Find and circle three things you can do.

P	R	A	Y	V	W	X	Y
Z	B	X	P	S	I	N	G
A	L	I	S	T	E	N	J

At Mass this Sunday, do these things to praise God and remember his great love for us.

PROJECT

Show What *you* Know

Write the two  in one sentence.

Mass

Eucharist

_____

_____

Question Corner

Pretend that you are with Jesus at the Last Supper. How does each statement make you feel?

Draw 😊 or 😞.	
This is my last meal with you.	◯
I give you the gift of myself.	◯
Remember me.	◯
I love you.	◯

DISCIPLE

Pray
Learn
Celebrate
Share
Choose
Live

What's *the* Word?

Remember what Jesus said at the Last Supper.

"Take and eat; this is my body."
(Matthew 26:26)

"Drink from it, all of you, for this is my blood." (Matthew 26:27–28)

Thank Jesus for all he has done for us.

Reality Check

When is Jesus with you?

❑ When I am at Mass

❑ When I celebrate Jesus' life

❑ When I pray with my parish

❑ Always

❑ Another time: _____

_____

Take Home

The most important thing our parish does is celebrate Mass together on Sunday. People of the parish give their time to help us celebrate. Talk with your family about who is at Mass to help celebrate the Eucharist. Make a list together.

_____

_____

193

Use the words in the box to complete the sentences.

parish

Eucharist

Mass

meal

priest

1. The Last Supper is the special

_____ that Jesus shared before he died.

2. The _____ is the sacrament of the Body and Blood of Jesus Christ.

3. The _____ is another name for the celebration of the Eucharist.

4. A _____ leads us in the celebration of the Mass.

5. We join with our _____ for the celebration of Mass.

 In what ways is Jesus with us during the celebration of Mass?

We Celebrate the Mass

WE GATHER

✝ **Leader:** Let us echo a song of praise to God.

Glory to God in the highest, (Echo) and on earth peace to people of good will. (Echo)

We praise you, (Echo)
we bless you, (Echo)
we adore you. (Echo)

☀ What are some ways you welcome people?

Glory to God

Glory to God

WE BELIEVE

We gather to worship God.

The Mass is the Church's greatest celebration. The most important time that our parish comes together is for Sunday Mass.

As we gather, we welcome one another. We stand and sing. With the priest, we pray the Sign of the Cross.
The priest says,
"The Lord be with you."
We answer together,
"And with your spirit."

Then we ask God and one another for forgiveness. We praise God by singing or praying aloud. Our prayer begins with these words: "Glory to God. . . ."

👤 Color the words that begin our prayer of praise.

Glory to God

We listen to God's Word.

The Bible is the book of God's Word. At Sunday Mass we listen to three readings from the Bible.

The first reading is about God's people who lived before Jesus Christ was born. The second reading is about the teachings of the Apostles. It is also about the beginning of the Church.

Next we stand and sing Alleluia or other words of praise. This shows we are ready to listen to the reading of the Gospel. The **Gospel** is the Good News about Jesus Christ and his teachings.

The priest or deacon reads the Gospel. Then he talks to us about all the readings. We learn how we can grow as followers of Jesus.

After the priest's talk, we stand. We say aloud what we believe as Catholics. Then we pray for the Church and all people.

 At Mass next Sunday listen carefully to the readings. Name ways we can show others that we have heard God's Word at Mass.

As Catholics...

The word *Gospel* means the "Good News of Jesus Christ." The Good News is that Jesus is the Son of God, who told us of God the Father's love.

Jesus taught us how to live. He died and rose to new life for us. This is the Good News we celebrate. What can you tell someone about the Good News of Jesus Christ?

Key Word

Gospel the Good News about Jesus Christ and his teachings

197

Our gifts of bread and wine become the Body and Blood of Christ.

The **altar** is the table of the Lord. The priest prepares the altar for the celebration of the Eucharist.

Everything we have is a gift from God. At the Eucharist we offer these gifts back to God. We offer ourselves, too. People bring gifts of bread and wine to the priest. The priest prepares the gifts of bread and wine. We pray, "Blessed be God for ever."

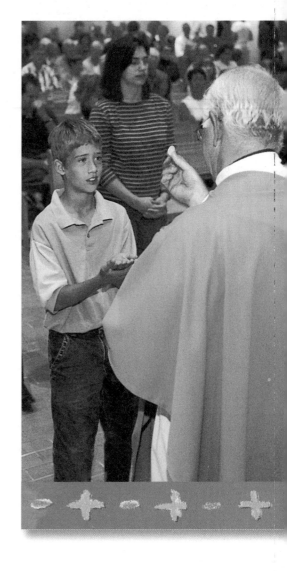

Read Along

We remember what Jesus said and did at the Last Supper. The priest takes the bread. He says,

"TAKE THIS, ALL OF YOU, AND EAT OF IT, FOR THIS IS MY BODY, WHICH WILL BE GIVEN UP FOR YOU."

Then the priest takes the cup of wine. He says,

"TAKE THIS, ALL OF YOU, AND DRINK FROM IT, FOR THIS IS THE CHALICE OF MY BLOOD . . ."

The bread and wine become the Body and Blood of Christ. This is done by the power of the Holy Spirit and through the words and actions of the priest. Jesus Christ is really present in the Eucharist.

We sing or pray, "Amen."
We are saying,
"Yes, I believe."

🎵 Sing **"Amen."**

We grow closer to Jesus and one another.

We get ready to receive Jesus by praying the Our Father. We share a sign of peace. Then we say a prayer to ask Jesus for forgiveness and peace.

The priest invites us to share in the Eucharist. The people who have received first Holy Communion receive the Body and Blood of Christ. They answer, "Amen."

While this is happening, we sing a song of thanks. This shows that we are joined with Jesus and the Church.

We quietly thank Jesus for the Eucharist.

After this the priest blesses us. We are sent out to live as Jesus' followers.

WE RESPOND

Write a way you can grow closer to Jesus.

_____

_____

Key Word

altar the table of the Lord

PROJECT

Show What you Know

Guess the **Key Word** for each riddle.

Gospel

altar

> The priest prepares me for the celebration of the Eucharist. I am the table of the Lord.

I am the _____.

> To show you are ready to listen to me, you stand and sing words of praise. I am the Good News about Jesus Christ and his teachings.

I am the _____.

 **Pray Today**

The prayers that the children are saying are from Sunday Mass.

Now, pass it on!

Lord, hear our prayer.

Thanks be to God.

Pray
Learn
Celebrate
Share
Choose
Live

What Would *you* do?

Imagine your friend asks you,
"What is the Good News about Jesus Christ?"

What would you say to
him or her? Write it in
the speech bubble.

Make *it* Happen

Do your best to participate
at Mass this Sunday!

Take Home

After Mass priests, deacons,
or extraordinary ministers
of Holy Communion take
the Eucharist to people who
cannot attend Mass because
they are sick. As a family, pray
for all those who are sick.

CHAPTER TEST

Circle the correct answer.

1. The altar is the _____ of the Lord.

   table   home

2. The _____ is the Good News about Jesus Christ and his teachings.

   Gospel   first reading

3. When we pray "Amen," we are saying, _____.

   "Yes, I believe"   "Forgive me"

4. When people receive the Body and Blood of Christ, they say _____.

   "Thank you"   "Amen"

5. We get ready to receive Jesus in Holy Communion by praying the _____.

   Our Father   Hail Mary

 What are some things we do at the beginning of Mass?

We Share God's Love

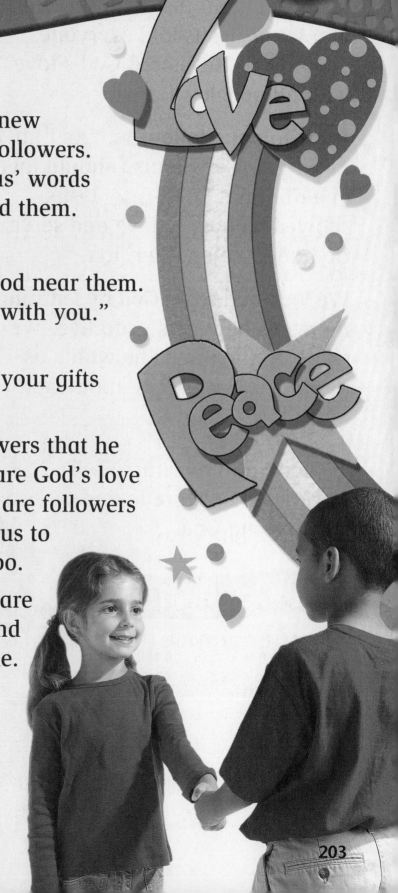

WE GATHER

✝ **Leader:** After Jesus rose to new life, he visited his followers. Let us listen to Jesus' words when he first visited them.

📖 John 20:19, 21

Reader: Jesus came and stood near them. He said, "Peace be with you."

(John 20:21)

All: Jesus, you gave us your gifts of peace and love.

Leader: Jesus told his followers that he wanted them to share God's love with everyone. We are followers of Jesus. He wants us to share God's love, too.

All: Jesus, help us to share your gifts of love and peace with everyone.

Were you ever asked to do something important? What were you asked?

WE BELIEVE

Jesus shows us how to love and serve.

Jesus did what his Father asked him to do. Jesus told everyone about God. He shared God's love with all people.

Jesus told his followers, "As I have loved you, so you also should love one another." (John 13:34) Jesus showed us how to love and serve God and one another, too.

We love and serve God by learning the ways he wants us to live. We try to do the things he wants us to do. We tell others about God and share his love.

Look at the picture. Tell how the people are loving and serving God.

As Catholics...

There are many ways to pray. We can praise God. We can tell God we are sorry for something we have done wrong. We can thank God for his loving care. We can ask God for what we need. We can pray for other people.

Try to pray in one or more of these ways today.

When we pray, we show God that we love him.

Prayer is listening to and talking to God. We grow closer to God when we pray.

Jesus taught us that God is his Father. He prayed to his Father often. He wants us to pray often, too. We pray to the Blessed Trinity: God the Father, God the Son, and God the Holy Spirit.

We can pray by ourselves. We can pray with our families, friends, and our parish. We can use our own words to pray. We can pray the prayers of the Church.

 Write a prayer that you will pray this week.

_____

_____

_____

_____

We share God's love with our families.

God wants us to love and serve him. We do this when we share God's love with our families in these ways.

- We are kind and helpful.

- We obey our parents and all those who care for us.

- We take care of the things that belong to our family.

- We show our love for all family members.

- We say we are sorry and forgive one another.

 Write one way your family shares God's love.

_____

_____

We share God's love with others.

God made each of us. He made us to share God's love with everyone. We can join with our own families to share God's love. We can join with members of our parish to do this, too.

WE RESPOND

Look at the pictures on these pages. Talk about what is happening in each picture. Tell how the people are loving and serving God.

🎵 **Walk in Love**

Walk in love as Jesus loved,
let us walk in Jesus,
light up the world,
light up the world
with God's own love.

PROJECT

Show What you Know

There is an important word missing from these statements. Write it in.

Jesus shows us how to _____ and serve.

When we pray, we show God that we _____ him.

We share God's _____ with our families.

We share God's _____ with others.

Make it Happen

Parish priests lead us in the celebration of the Eucharist. They help us prepare to celebrate the other sacraments. They visit people who are sick. They help people learn more about the Bible and the Church. As a class, write a card to your parish priest to thank him for serving God and others.

Pray
Learn
Celebrate
Share
Choose
Live

Picture This

Draw a picture of:

a way that you show your family members you love them	a way that you show God you love him

↳ **DISCIPLE CHALLENGE** How are these ways alike? How are they different?

Take Home

Invite each member of your family to complete the following. Write your initials beside one thing you will do to share God's love with your family this week.

- I will be kind and helpful.
- I will obey my parents.
- I will take care of things that belong to my family.
- I will forgive others.

Circle the correct answer.

1. Do we serve God when we show others his love?

Yes   **No**

2. Do we share God's love with our family members when we take things that belong to them?

Yes   **No**

3. Do we share God's love when we forgive one another?

Yes   **No**

4. Did Jesus tell everyone about God?

Yes   **No**

5. Is there only one way to pray?

Yes   **No**

 How do we share God's love with our families?

We Honor Mary and the Saints

WE GATHER

✝ **Leader:** God chose Mary to be the Mother of his own Son, Jesus. Listen to God's Word.

 Luke 1: 26–28, 35

Read Along

Before Jesus was born, God sent an angel to Mary. The angel said to Mary, "Hail, favored one! The Lord is with you." (Luke 1:28) The angel told Mary that she was going to have a son. The angel told her, "The child to be born will be called holy, the Son of God." (Luke 1:35)

Leader: Joseph was Mary's husband. He loved and cared for Mary and Jesus.

🎵 Joseph Was a Good Man

Joseph was a good man,
a good man, a good man,
Joseph was a good man,
chosen by the Lord.
And Joseph loved a lady,
Joseph loved a lady,
Joseph loved a lady,
chosen by the Lord.

☀ How do we honor people? Name someone you would like to honor.

WE BELIEVE

Mary is the mother of Jesus.

God asked Mary to be the Mother of his Son. Mary said "yes" to God. Mary gave birth to God's only Son, Jesus.

Mary loved Jesus. Mary cared for him. She helped him learn many things.

Mary listened to Jesus teach. She watched him heal the sick. She celebrated special times with him.

Jesus always loved his mother. He wanted his followers to love and care for her, too. Mary shows us how to live as Jesus asks us to.

 Write a sentence to tell about the picture.

_____

_____

The Church honors Mary.

The Church honors Mary because she is the mother of Jesus. To show our love, we call her "Our Lady" and "The Blessed Mother."

We honor Mary as the Mother of the Church. We celebrate her feast days. On these days, we remember special times in the lives of Mary and Jesus.

The Church also has prayers to honor Mary. One special prayer is the Hail Mary.

Pray the Hail Mary together.

Hail Mary, full of grace,
the Lord is with you!
Blessed are you among women,
and blessed is the fruit of your
    womb, Jesus.
Holy Mary, Mother of God,
pray for us sinners,
now and at the hour of our death.
Amen.

As Catholics...

We honor Mary in a special way on certain days of the year. On some of these days, parishes gather together for processions. On these special prayer walks, the people sing songs to Mary and pray special prayers. They put flowers in front of a statue of Mary. In this way they honor Mary.

Find out ways your parish honors Mary.

The saints are close to God.

The **saints** are followers of Jesus who have died and now live forever with God. The saints tried to live the way Jesus asked. They loved God very much. They put God first in their lives. They tried to share God's love with others. They prayed to God often.

Look at the pictures on these pages. They show some saints of the Church. Read the sentence below each picture.

Use a yellow crayon. Highlight each saint's name. Talk about some people you know who do the things these saints did.

Saint John Vianney was a parish priest who served his people.

Saint Teresa of Avila wrote books and letters to help people love Jesus.

Saint Andrew Kim Taegon was the first priest and pastor in Korea.

Saint Francis Xavier taught the people of India to know God.

saints followers of Jesus who have died and now live forever with God

214

We honor all the saints of the Church.

There are many, many saints. All the saints loved God very much.

The Church has a special day to honor all the saints. We call this day the Feast of All Saints. This day is November 1.

On this day we celebrate Mass with our parish family. We thank God for all the saints.

All through the year, we can ask the saints to pray for us. We can ask them to help us grow close to God. We can honor them by trying to be more like them.

WE RESPOND

Tell some ways we can be like the saints. Ask the saints to pray for us.

🎵 When the Saints Go Marching In

Oh, when the saints
   go marching in.
Oh, when the saints
   go marching in.
Oh, Lord, how I want to be in that number,
when the saints go marching in.

Saint Katharine Drexel began schools for Native American and African American children.

Saint Anne was the mother of Mary and the grandmother of Jesus.

PROJECT

Show What you Know

Unscramble the Key Word.

t a s i n s _____ _____ _____ _____ _____ _____

↳ **DISCIPLE CHALLENGE** What does the Key Word mean?

_____

Picture This   Draw a way you can honor your mother. Then, draw a way you can honor Mary.

How are these ways alike? How are they different?

DISCIPLE

Pray
Learn
Celebrate
Share
Choose
Live

Saint Stories

Saint Joseph was the husband of Mary and foster father of Jesus. He cared for them. He worked as a carpenter. We can ask Saint Joseph to help all the workers of the world. We celebrate the Feast of Saint Joseph the Worker on May 1.

Hail Mary

Make it Happen

Jesus wants us to love his mother Mary. We can show our love by praying to her. Decorate the first words of this prayer.

More to Explore

Many people are named after a saint. Are you? Learn about this saint or another saint that interests you. Visit the library or *Lives of the Saints* at www.webelieveweb.com.

Take Home

Family was very important to Jesus. He and Mary and Joseph loved and cared for one another. Who loves and cares for you? Make a family tree. Include your family members. Talk about your family tree.

CHAPTER TEST

Circle the correct answer.

1. Mary is the _____ of Jesus.

mother   sister

2. A special prayer we honor Mary with is the _____.

Our Father   Hail Mary

3. _____ are followers of Jesus who have died and now live forever with God.

Saints   Sacraments

4. There are _____ saints.

many   just a few

5. The saints are _____ God.

far away from   close to

 What are some of the things we do to honor Mary?

We Care for the Gifts of God's Creation

WE GATHER

✝ **Leader:** Close your eyes and sit quietly. Think about all the gifts of God's creation. Now let us praise God for all these gifts.

🎵 **Shout from the Mountains**

Shout from the mountains,
Sing in the valleys,
Call from the waters,
Dance through the hills!
All of God's people,
All of God's creatures,
All of creation,
Join in the song!

And we sing:
Holy, holy, holy is God!
Holy, holy, holy and strong!

☀ What is your favorite outdoor place? What do you see there?

WE BELIEVE

The world is God's gift to us.

God has given us all of creation to use and enjoy. The world is full of beautiful places and wonderful plants and animals.

God asks us to take care of his creation. God wants people everywhere to be able to use these gifts. God wants us to share these gifts of creation.

Tell how the people in the pictures are taking care of creation. Circle each picture that shows what you can do.

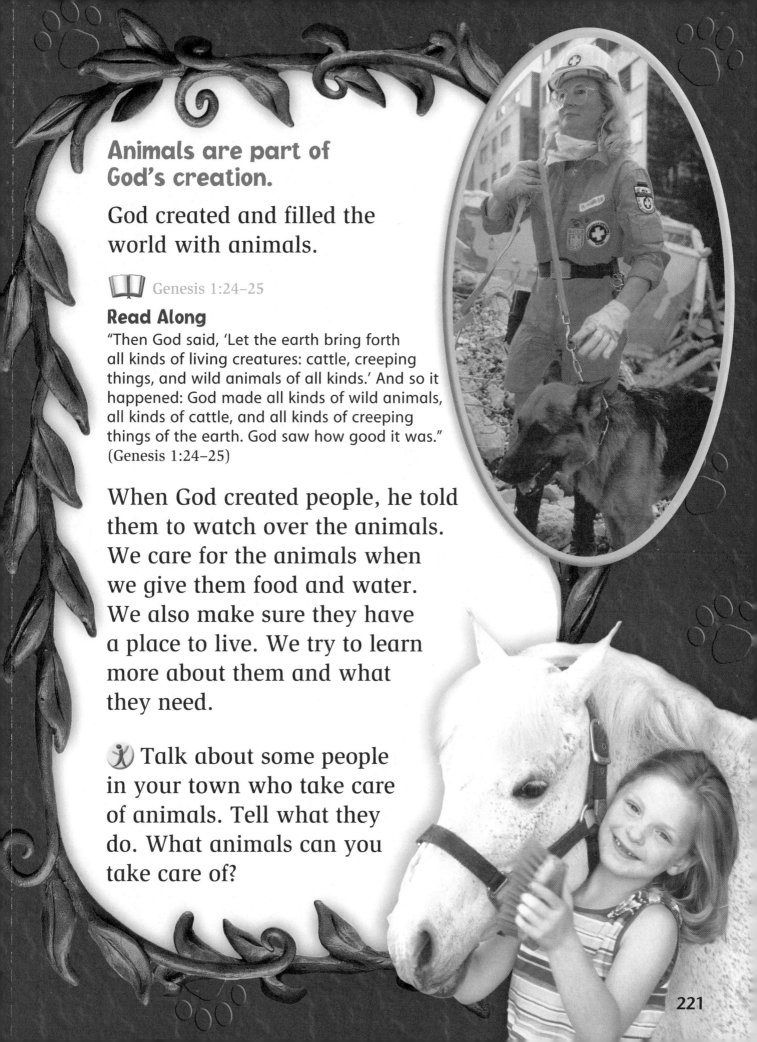

Animals are part of God's creation.

God created and filled the world with animals.

📖 Genesis 1:24–25

Read Along

"Then God said, 'Let the earth bring forth all kinds of living creatures: cattle, creeping things, and wild animals of all kinds.' And so it happened: God made all kinds of wild animals, all kinds of cattle, and all kinds of creeping things of the earth. God saw how good it was." (Genesis 1:24–25)

When God created people, he told them to watch over the animals. We care for the animals when we give them food and water. We also make sure they have a place to live. We try to learn more about them and what they need.

🧍 Talk about some people in your town who take care of animals. Tell what they do. What animals can you take care of?

We are all important to God.

God created each one of us. No two people in the world are exactly alike. We enjoy different things. We have different gifts and talents. We look different from each other.

God wants us to use our gifts and talents. We can use them to take care of creation and to care for one another.

Think about what your special gifts are. Draw a picture to show a way you can share one gift.

As Catholics...

Each of us is special. God loves each and every one of us. He gave us the gift of life. We can show God our thanks for the gift of life. One way we can do this is by taking care of ourselves. We can take care of ourselves by:

- eating the right foods
- getting enough sleep
- keeping ourselves clean
- obeying rules.

What other ways can we thank God for the gift of life?

We care for and respect all people.

Jesus often talked about ways we should treat other people.

 Matthew 7:12

Read Along

Jesus said, "Do to others whatever you would have them do to you." (Matthew 7:12)

Jesus meant that we should treat other people the way we want to be treated. We should show kindness and respect. We should share God's love with all people. Here are some ways we can do this.

- Respect other people's belongings. Do not take anything without asking.
- Tell the truth. Do not tell lies.
- Ask for forgiveness if we have done something wrong.
- Forgive other people when they tell us they are sorry.

WE RESPOND

Let us thank God for making all people.

🎵 **Malo! Malo! Thanks Be to God**

(Sing each line two times)

Malo! Malo!
Thanks be to God!
O-bri-ga-do!
Alleluia!
Gra-ci-as!
Kam-sa-ham-ni-da!
Malo! Malo!
Thanks be to God!

PROJECT

Show What *you* Know

Describe God's creation.
Use words or pictures.

Reality Check

Today I can share God's love by

❏ being polite.

❏ telling lies.

❏ taking others' belongings without asking.

❏ asking for forgiveness.

❏ forgiving others.

DISCIPLE

Pray
Learn
Celebrate
Share
Choose
Live

Question Corner

Every person is special to God. You are special to God. Share your story. Draw a picture of yourself. Answer the questions below.

What makes you a disciple of Jesus?

_____

What is a special gift you have from God?

_____

How can you help take care of God's creation?

_____

_____

Take Home

Talk together about ways you can help care for God's creation as a family.

Use the words in the box to complete the sentences.

respect

treat

created

gift

animals

1. The world is God's

_____ to all people.

2. God told people to watch over the

_____ he created.

3. All people in the world are

_____ by God.

4. Jesus told us to _____ others
the way we want to be treated.

5. Jesus wants us to treat all people with kindness

and _____.

 How can we share God's love with
other people?

"This is the day the LORD has made;
let us rejoice in it and be glad."

Psalm 118:24

SEASONAL
CHAPTER 27

This chapter celebrates the entire
Easter season.

227

The Church celebrates that Jesus rose to new life.

WE GATHER

What are some signs of new life? Share your ideas with one another.

WE BELIEVE

Easter is a time of great joy. The Three Days lead us to Easter Sunday. It is time to rejoice!

During Mass on Easter Sunday, we listen to the story of Jesus' rising from the dead. Here is what Saint Matthew tells us.

 Matthew 28:1–10

Narrator: "After the sabbath, as the first day of the week was dawning, Mary Magdalene and the other Mary came to see the tomb. And behold, there was a great earthquake; for an angel of the Lord descended from heaven, approached, rolled back the stone, and sat upon it." (Matthew 28:1–2)

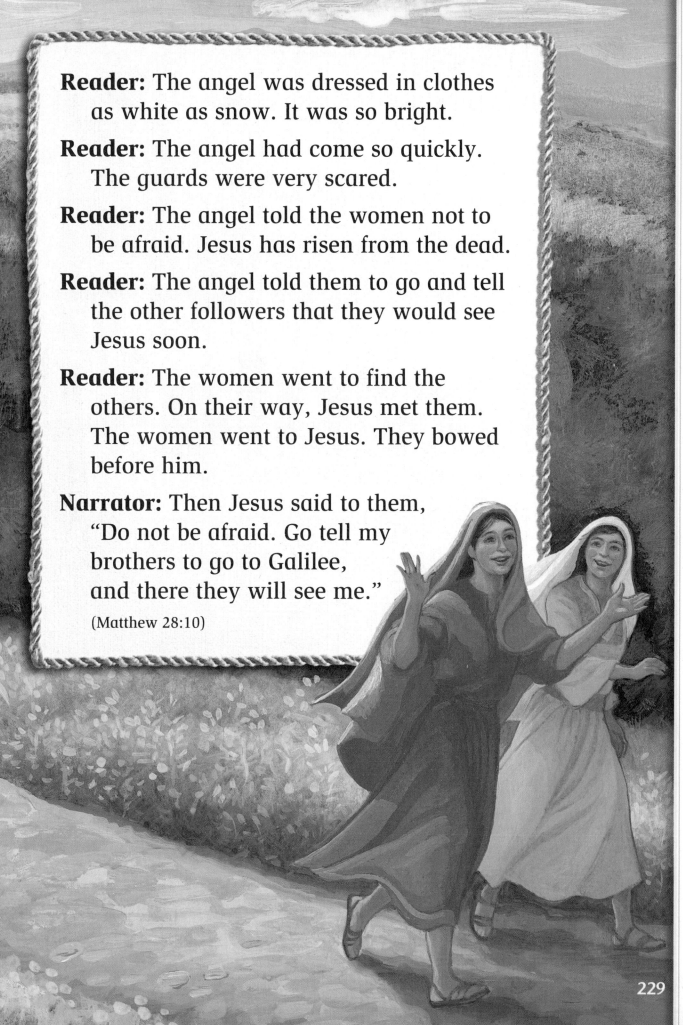

Reader: The angel was dressed in clothes as white as snow. It was so bright.

Reader: The angel had come so quickly. The guards were very scared.

Reader: The angel told the women not to be afraid. Jesus has risen from the dead.

Reader: The angel told them to go and tell the other followers that they would see Jesus soon.

Reader: The women went to find the others. On their way, Jesus met them. The women went to Jesus. They bowed before him.

Narrator: Then Jesus said to them, "Do not be afraid. Go tell my brothers to go to Galilee, and there they will see me."

(Matthew 28:10)

During Easter we celebrate that Jesus rose to new life.

Decorate the Alleluia banner with signs of new life.

Alleluia!

✞ We Respond in Prayer

Leader: Praised be the risen Jesus.

All: Let us rejoice and be glad, alleluia!

🎵 **Alleluia No. 1**

Chorus
> Alleluia, alleluia!
> Give thanks to the risen
>   Lord.
> Alleluia, alleluia!
> Give praise to his name.

> Spread the good news o'er
>   all the earth:
> Jesus has died and has risen. (Chorus)

PROJECT DISCIPLE

Celebrate!

Use the code to discover an important message.

J	R	E	O	I	C	S	U	D	A	N	R	T	W	L	F
1	2	3	4	5	6	7	8	9	10	11	12	13	14	15	16

__ __ __ __ __ __ __ ! __ __ __ __ __
2 3 1 4 5 6 3   1 3 7 8 7

__ __ __ __ __ __ __ __ __ __ __
9 5 3 9   10 11 9   2 4 7 3

__ __ __ __ __ __ __ __ __ !
13 4   11 3 14   15 5 16 3

Fast Facts

Eggs are a symbol of new life. So eggs are a symbol of Easter too! At Easter Jesus rose to new life.

Take Home

With your family list ways that you celebrate Easter together.

UNIT TEST

Circle the correct answer.

1. Is the Eucharist the sacrament of the Body and Blood of Jesus Christ?　　**Yes**　　**No**

2. Does Jesus want us to treat people unfairly?　　**Yes**　　**No**

3. Do we call the celebration of the Eucharist the Mass?　　**Yes**　　**No**

4. Did the saints put God last in their lives?　　**Yes**　　**No**

5. Does the Church honor Mary in different ways?　　**Yes**　　**No**

Write the correct word to finish each sentence.

6. The _____ is the Church's greatest celebration.

7. The _____ are followers of Jesus who have died and now live forever with God.

8. The _____ is the table of the Lord.

altar

saints

Mass

continued on next page

9. Choose and circle one of the pictures. Write how the people are sharing God's love.

_____

10. Write sentences to tell a few ways you can share God's love.

_____

_____

_____

_____

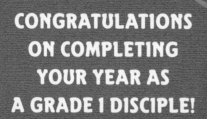

CONGRATULATIONS ON COMPLETING YOUR YEAR AS A GRADE 1 DISCIPLE!

Fold on this line.

PROJECT DISCIPLE LOG

Pray
Learn
Celebrate
Share
Choose
Live

A RECORD OF MY JOURNEY AS A GRADE 1 DISCIPLE

_____
Name

✂ Cut on this line.

Disciples of Jesus listen to and share God's Word.

My picture of my favorite story about Jesus

Disciples of Jesus pray every day.

A prayer I learned this year is

_____.

I pray this prayer

❏ by myself

❏ with my family

❏ with my classmates

❏ with my parish.

My prayer for summer is

_____.

4

5

Disciples of Jesus learn about their faith.

One thing I learned this year
- about following Jesus is

_____ .

- about sharing my faith with others is

_____ .

2

Disciples of Jesus live out their faith.

This summer I will live out my faith when I am
- ❑ with my family
- ❑ with my friends
- ❑ on vacation
- ❑ on day trips
- ❑ in my neighborhood
- ❑ in church

❑ _____ .

7

Disciples of Jesus make loving choices.

This year I made a loving choice
- to care for God's world by

_____ .

- to help my family by

_____ .

This summer, I can show love for others by

_____ .

6

Disciples of Jesus celebrate the Church year.

My favorite time of the Church year was

_____ .

I celebrated with

_____ .

We celebrated by

_____ .

3

End-of-Year Prayer Service

✝ We Gather in Prayer

Leader: We have learned many things about God this year.

Group 1: God is our loving Father.

Group 2: God sent his own Son, Jesus, to us.

Group 3: God shares his life and love with us.

Group 4: God wants us to share his love with others.

Leader: God, we want to remember all of these good things.

All: God, thank you for all your wonderful gifts. We believe that you are with us always. We want to share your love with others this summer.

🎵 We Celebrate With Joy

We celebrate with joy and gladness
We celebrate God's love for us.
We celebrate with joy and gladness.
God with us today.
God with us today.

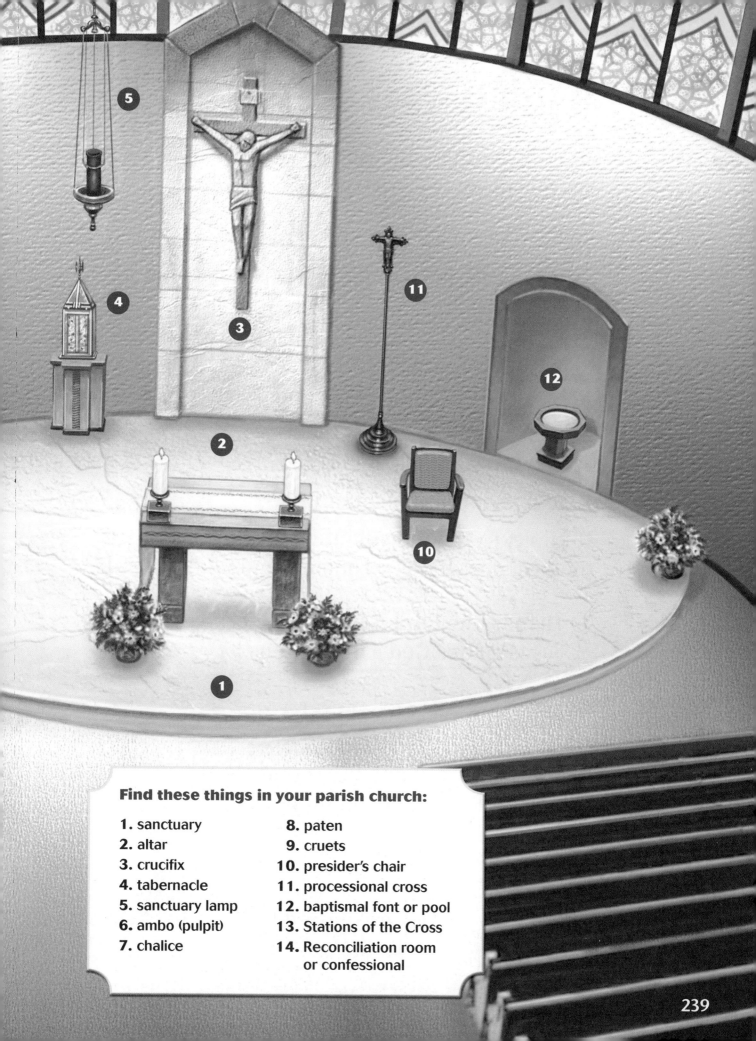

Find these things in your parish church:

1. sanctuary
2. altar
3. crucifix
4. tabernacle
5. sanctuary lamp
6. ambo (pulpit)
7. chalice
8. paten
9. cruets
10. presider's chair
11. processional cross
12. baptismal font or pool
13. Stations of the Cross
14. Reconciliation room or confessional

PROJECT DISCIPLE

You are learning and living out ways to be a disciple of Jesus Christ.

Look what awaits you in:

We Believe Grade 2: Jesus Shares God's Life.

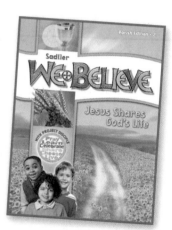

You will learn about and live out that

- Jesus Christ is with us always.
- Jesus calls us to Penance and Reconciliation.
- Jesus gives himself in the Eucharist.
- We live our Catholic faith.

Until next year, pay attention each time you go to Mass. Look around you. Listen.

Here is one thing I know about the ways Jesus shares God's life with us.

_____

Here is one thing that I want to learn more about next year.

_____

We are blessed to share in God's life!

My
Mass
Book

Fold on this line.

Cut on this line.

The priest blesses us. The priest or deacon may say, "Go in peace."
We say,

"Thanks be to God."

We go out to live as Jesus' followers.

We welcome one another. We stand and sing. We pray the Sign of the Cross. The priest says, "The Lord be with you."
We answer,

"And with your spirit."

We gather with our parish. We remember and celebrate what Jesus said and did at the Last Supper.

Fold on this line.

Cut on this line.

We ask God and one another for forgiveness. We praise God as we sing,

"Glory to God in the highest, and on earth peace to people of good will."

Then the priest invites us to share in the Eucharist. As people receive the Body and Blood of Christ, they answer,

"Amen."

While this is happening, we sing a song of thanks.

We get ready to receive Jesus. Together we pray or sing the Our Father. Then we share a sign of peace. We say,

"Peace be with you."

Fold on this line.

Cut on this line.

We listen to two readings from the Bible. After each one, the reader says, "The word of the Lord." We answer,

"Thanks be to God."

Then the priest takes the cup of wine. He says, "Take this, all of you, and drink from it, for this is the chalice of my Blood. . . ."

We stand to say aloud what we believe as Catholics. Then we pray for the Church and all people. After each prayer we say,

"Lord, hear our prayer."

We stand and sing **Alleluia.**

The priest or deacon reads the Gospel. Then he says, "The Gospel of the Lord." We answer,

"Praise to you, Lord Jesus Christ."

We sing or pray,

"Amen."

We believe Jesus Christ is really present in the Eucharist.

The priest prepares the altar. People bring gifts of bread and wine to the priest. The priest prepares these gifts. We pray,

"Blessed be God for ever."

Then we remember what Jesus said and did at the Last Supper. The priest takes the bread. He says, "TAKE THIS, ALL OF YOU, AND EAT OF IT, FOR THIS IS MY BODY, WHICH WILL BE GIVEN UP FOR YOU."

Fold on this line.

Cut on this line.

My Prayer Book

Angel of God

Angel of God,
my guardian dear,
to whom God's love commits
    me here,
ever this day be at my side,
to light and guard, to rule
    and guide.

Amen.

Glory Be to the Father

Glory be to the Father
and to the Son
and to the Holy Spirit,
as it was in the beginning
is now, and ever shall be
world without end.

Amen.

Sign of the Cross

In the name of the Father,
and of the Son,
and of the Holy Spirit.

Amen.

Fold on this line.

✂ Cut on this line.

Act of Contrition

Read Along

My God,
I am sorry for my sins with all my heart.
In choosing to do wrong
and failing to do good,
I have sinned against you
whom I should love above all things.
I firmly intend, with your help,
to do penance,
to sin no more,
and to avoid whatever leads me to sin.
Our Savior Jesus Christ
suffered and died for us.
In his name, my God, have mercy.

Our Father

Our Father, who art
  in heaven,
hallowed be thy name;
thy kingdom come;
thy will be done on earth
  as it is in heaven.

he ascended into heaven,
  and is seated at the right hand
  of God the Father almighty;
from there he will come to judge
  the living and the dead.

I believe in the Holy Spirit,
  the holy catholic Church,
  the communion of saints,
  the forgiveness of sins,
  the resurrection of the body,
  and life everlasting.

Amen.

The Apostles' Creed

Read Along

I believe in God,
the Father almighty,
Creator of heaven and earth,

and in Jesus Christ,
his only Son, our Lord,
who was conceived by
the Holy Spirit,
born of the Virgin Mary,
suffered under Pontius Pilate,
was crucified, died and
was buried;
he descended into hell;
on the third day he rose again
from the dead;

Fold on this line.

Cut on this line.

Give us this day our
daily bread;
and forgive us our
trespasses
as we forgive those who
trespass against us;
and lead us not into
temptation,
but deliver us from evil.

Amen.

Grace Before Meals

Bless us, O Lord, and these
your gifts
which we are about
to receive
from your goodness.
Through Christ our Lord.

Amen.

Holy Mary, Mother of God,
pray for us sinners,
now and at the hour of
our death.

Amen.

Hail Mary

Hail Mary, full of grace,
the Lord is with you!
Blessed are you among
   women,
and blessed is the fruit of
   your womb, Jesus.

Grace After Meals

We give you thanks
   almighty God
for these and all your gifts,
which we have received
   through
Christ our Lord.

Amen.

6

11

Morning Offering

My God, I offer you today
all that I think and do
   and say,
uniting it with what
   was done
on earth, by Jesus Christ,
your Son.

Evening Prayer

Dear God, before I sleep
I want to thank you for
   this day
so full of your kindness
and your joy.
I close my eyes to rest
safe in your loving care.

The Seven Sacraments

The Sacraments of Christian Initiation
Baptism
Confirmation
Eucharist

The Sacraments of Healing
Penance and Reconciliation
Anointing of the Sick

The Sacraments at the Service of Communion
Holy Orders
Matrimony

The Ten Commandments

1. I am the LORD your God: you shall not have strange gods before me.

2. You shall not take the name of the LORD your God in vain.

3. Remember to keep holy the LORD's Day.

4. Honor your father and your mother.

5. You shall not kill.

6. You shall not commit adultery.

7. You shall not steal.

8. You shall not bear false witness against your neighbor.

9. You shall not covet your neighbor's wife.

10. You shall not covet your neighbor's goods.

Glossary

altar (page 199)
the table of the Lord

Apostles (page 76)
twelve men Jesus chose to
lead his followers

Baptism (page 149)
the sacrament in which we
become children of God and
members of the Church

Bible (page 21)
the book of God's Word

Blessed Trinity (page 31)
One God in Three Persons:
God the Father, God the Son, and
God the Holy Spirit

Christmas (page 37)
the time when we celebrate the
birth of God's Son, Jesus

Church (page 101)
all the people who believe in Jesus
and follow his teachings

Lord's Prayer (page 78)
the prayer Jesus taught his followers

Mass (page 191)
another name for the celebration of the Eucharist

parish (page 133)
a group of Catholics who join together to share God's love

pastor (page 134)
the priest who is the leader of the parish

peacemaker (page 158)
a person who works for peace

Penance and Reconciliation (page 166)
the sacrament in which we receive and celebrate God's forgiveness

Pentecost (page 95)
the day the Holy Spirit came to Jesus' followers

prayer (page 31)
listening and talking to God

sacrament (page 142)
a special sign given to us by Jesus

saints (page 214)
followers of Jesus who have died
and now live forever with God

Sign of the Cross (page 31)
a prayer to the Blessed Trinity

Temple (page 87)
the holy place in Jerusalem where
the Jewish People prayed

trust (page 46)
to believe in someone's love for us

worship (page 133)
to give God thanks and praise

Index

The following is a list of topics that appear in the pupil's text.
Boldface indicates an entire chapter.